M000251710

Ancestors Through My Eyes

by
Karen Kiaer

Ancestors Through My Eyes
The Story of an American Family

Copyright ©2018 Karen Kiaer

ISBN 978-0-692-12057-6

All rights reserved. No part of this publication may be reproduced, distributed, or transmitted in any form or by any means, including photocopying, recording, or other electronic or mechanical methods, without the prior written permission of the publisher, except in the case of brief quotations embodied in critical reviews and certain other noncommercial uses permitted by copyright law.

Cover design by Vanessa King

Book design by StoriesToTellBooks.com

Ancestors Through My Eyes

by
Karen Kiaer

THE STORY OF AN AMERICAN FAMILY
THE INGERSOLLS OF MASSACHUSETTS, NEW YORK, & MICHIGAN: 1620-1920

CONTENTS

For generations past

Those at present: Lisa, Edward, John, Scott, Lucas & Sofia

And generations yet to come

PREFACE

As my family's self-designated genealogist, having finished a memoir, I thought about looking outside the insular family in which I was raised. My California grandmother, whom I called "Cracker" and with whom I was close, often spoke about our English ancestor John Ingersoll. I read her mother's well-worn 1926 copy of A Genealogy of the Ingersoll Family in America. This was written by Lillian Drake Avery, a Michigan-born Daughter of the American Revolution (DAR). Avery's investigation into the history of the Ingersoll family was part of her application to join the DAR and was another factor in my desire to determine my own genealogy. This is my effort to uncover ten generations of my Ingersoll line and the historical circumstances in which they found themselves. To share this "American" history with my children, grandchildren, Ingersoll descendants, DAR Daughters, SAR Sons and all those interested in uncovering "their story."

Research for the book took me to western Massachusetts, upstate New York and the hilly farmlands of southwestern Michigan. I visited rural historical societies and small-town libraries, and spent many hours on the internet. I followed clues and tracks left by the Ingersoll's ten generations, which included uncovering centuries-old historical land transfers, sleeping in old homesteads, navigating through microfiche and delicate diaries, reading Last Wills and Testaments, and standing in burial grounds, many, many graveyards, to place my hands on ancient gravestones.

What follows covers a period of American history from approximately 1626 to 1946, seen through my eyes. American history is complex, and for much of its history, problematic. In the eras the Ingersolls traveled to America and built their homes, the destruction of the indigenous people and their world through violence and savagery marked the founding and evolution of England's North American colonies. This affected the first seven generations of Ingersolls. I found a history fraught with land dispossession and massacre but also innovation, bravery, risk-taking and a godly people.

Leaving Massachusetts and New York, I followed the next several generations of Ingersolls to Michigan, and finally California, to shed light on the influences of religion, conflict and socioeconomic trends on the family, from the early Massachusetts settlements through the American Revolution and Civil War into the twentieth century.

I have included a bibliography, images, websites and the names of organizations I found germane to my specific Ingersoll family research. I trust it serves as a model for all those curious sleuths of history who wish to discover the stories of their families. Given the breadth and details of nearly three hundred years of American history, I have mainly concentrated on western Massachusetts and southwestern Michigan. If I have omitted any pertinent facts or misstated any information, please feel free to correct me. This was a labor of love driven by curiosity and the desire to discover my own history.

INTRODUCTION

The Ingersoll Crest
"Virtue lives but fame dies"

I begin the Ingersoll story in Westfield, Massachusetts. A town remembered as the "whip" capital of America during its manufacturing nineteenth-century heyday – a manufacturing town where all kinds of whips were produced for horse-drawn carriages and their coachmen. Today, Westfield, a town of forty thousand people, is the poor cousin to the more sophisticated Berkshire tourist towns of Stockbridge and Great Barrington. In 1651, however, it was the most western settlement in the state where ten families "planted" themselves one hundred miles from Puritan Boston. John Ingersoll and his third wife, Mary Hunt Webster, were one of those ten families. They are my first generation English ancestors.

After three hours of perusing documents in the Westfield Athenaeum, I found both John and Mary Ingersoll on an updated Town Cemetery List: plot A, section A, 1684 and 1690. But why, I wondered, was there a question mark after their names? I also found an onionskin map of the early settlers' homesteads showing the Ingersoll family with a plot on the Little River in Westfield, bounded by the Dewey family to the east and the Phelps family on the west. I decided to visit the old burial ground on Mechanic Street in Westfield to find John and Mary, but I needed a guide.

Knowing marriages between these families took place from previous research, and having the afternoon free, I looked up Dewey and Phelps in the local phone book. I found a listing for Robert G. Dewey of Tanner Lane, Westfield. I dialed the phone number and was greeted by the firm voice of Robert Dewey Sr.

"Is this the Robert Dewey of the Little River Dewey Family?" I asked.

"Yes, I'm Robert Dewey, a descendent of the first Little River Dewey family."

"Robert, I believe we are related through marriage. A Dewey married an Ingersoll ancestor of mine in the second generation."

"Yes, we're probably related. I know the Westfield history inside and out. I was born and raised here. My family has been here since the mid 1600's."

The conversation continued and Robert Dewey offered to give me a tour of the old burial ground that very afternoon.

"Do you know where in the burial ground your folks are?"

"No, there is a question mark next to John and Mary's names, but there is location information for their son Thomas, his wives Sarah Dewey and Sarah Ashley and several other family members."

"We'll find them," a confident Dewey replied.

At 2 p.m. on a sunny October afternoon, Robert met me with his divining rod at the entrance of the Mechanic Street Cemetery. He was a short, erect man with silver-white hair parted down the right side.

"I'm eighty-four," he admitted, "but still in good shape with a little Yankee good humor left."

Following Robert to the oldest section in the cemetery, armed with string and markers, I watched Robert isolate and mark out a four- by four-foot grassy area of seventeen century, two-feet-high, curved and chiseled stones. Barely legible, the names read: Root, Phelps, Dewey, Ashley and Ingersoll. After an hour of probing, he felt the broken-off rock base of what he was sure was the original gravestone of John and Mary Ingersoll.

"It's missing," said Robert. "But this is the base, I'm sure."

Finding the "missing" stone base, but not the missing headstone, my sleuth instincts shifted into high gear. Unearth the story!

CHAPTER 1

FIRST GENERATION
Massachusetts

John Ingersoll 1626-1684
Mary Webster Hunt 1640-1690

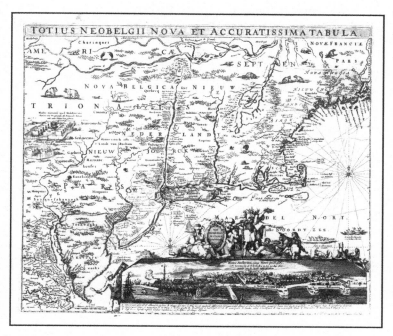

Early 1600 New England Map

FAMILIES OF JOHN INGERSOLL

First Wife: Dorothy Lord (1629-1657)

Children

Hannah Ingersoll (1652-1714)
Dorothy Ingersoll (1654-1672)
Margery Ingersoll (1656-1697)

Second Wife: Abigail Bascom (1640-1666)

Children

Abigail Ingersoll (1658-1727)
Sarah Ingersoll (1660-1712)
Abiah Ingersoll (1663-1732)
Hester Ingersoll (1665-1732)

Third Wife: Mary Webster Hunt (1639-1690)

Children

Thomas Ingersoll (1668-1732)
John Ingersoll (1671-1745)
Ebenezer Ingersoll (1673-1682)
Joseph Ingersoll (1675-1704)
Mary Ingersoll (1677-1690)
Benjamin Ingersoll (1679-1704)
Jonathan Ingersoll (1681-1760)

John Ingersoll I

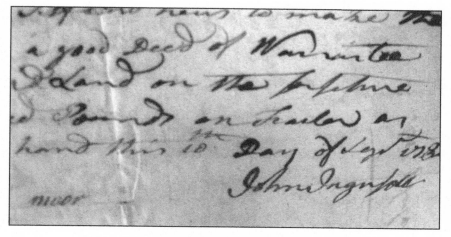

Signature – Westfield Athenaeum Archives

John Ingersoll was born in Derby, England in 1626. His father, Thomas, worked as a shoemaker and town crier; John's mother was Margery Eaton. Thomas would leave Derby for London to work for the Stepney Parish on the Thames as a "roper" in the shipbuilding industry. A roper was a craftsman who made braided rope (cordage) for ships' riggings, a higher paid craft much sought after. Outbreaks of plague in London often sent the Ingersoll family back to the safety of the nearby Derby countryside.

John was eighteen during the reign of Charles II. It was the England of Shakespeare, where all ranks of people loved words, plays, music and sermons, or lectures as they were called in that time. Lectures were given daily in various churches and attended by all. John's church was St. Warburg's in Derby. He'd listen to the words of the preacher, turning every word over in his head. We know this from writings John did, as was the custom. "The inclination of men is to know the truth about God and to live in communities," John wrote, as had been pronounced by preacher Thomas Hooker.

At the time, a gentleman's son usually served an apprenticeship. Beginning at age fourteen, John was sent to London to apprentice with Thomas Dawes of the London firm, Tyler and Bricklayers Company. Spending years as an apprentice meant years of service in a transitory status, bound to a trade. To come out of his indenture was to become a journeyman for life and to marry a master's daughter. That was the usual life of a working man. John thought that it would be better to cross the ocean to the New World, where it was thought economic opportunity lay. While visiting his ill father in Derby in 1644, John discussed his desire to go to America. His opportunity came in 1649 when his master, William Dawes, told John he was planning on leaving for America and asked if John wanted to accompany him.

This wasn't unusual for the times. It was customary for young men to travel and immigrate, and it was looked upon as normal for that age. Life expectancy was only thirty to thirty-five years, and the men were anxious to leave behind the plagues, famines, squalid housing conditions and wars. Even the price of firewood had increased, due to the housing and shipping boom of the 1630's. In addition to lectures of parish ministers, there were propaganda, pamphlets, advertisements and personal correspondence – all promoting colonization. The Massachusetts Bay Company, a private trading company made up of wealthy merchants and businessmen armed with land grants and patents from the king, funded the trips. They were a Bible commonwealth of a few dozen oligarchs and aristocrats who would govern, rule and tax an under-franchised majority.

John made the seven-week, three-thousand-mile ocean crossing on an English square-rigged merchant ship. It was a fifty-foot wooden vessel with nearly two hundred people cramped together with their livestock, little privacy or sanitation, rife with seasickness and small-pox. Meals, provided by the ship's owners, commonly consisted of salted beef, pork, fish and "hardtack," a hard dry biscuit, supple-mented by families who brought goats for milk for their children.

John left a decade of English civil war. He traveled with men of common beliefs and shared dreams. They arrived in Boston about 1649 and found the streets bustling with construction, busy shops, brickworks and wharves with ropewalks turning out cordage made from hemp.

I don't know the name of the ship John traveled to America on. For over two hundred years, non-family researchers have suggested that John traveled with his older brother Richard and others, as well as with his employer Thomas Dawes.

Migration crossings were family affairs, and youths like John who did not travel with their immediate families, crossed with a household, often cousins or families from their hometowns. Ship and port logs of seventeenth century crossings have been transcribed by scholars, but many lists have been lost or destroyed, and many passengers who did not get the necessary travel permits and permission from the Crown, used false names. My research led me to Dawes. Thomas Dawes left England for America in 1649 when John would have been twenty-three-years old. This date seems more plausible than 1629, as some records show, since John would have been three! Records show John in Hartford in 1651, where he married his first wife, Dorothy Lord. There is also a record from a Connecticut court dated 1654, stating he was "... fined 10s ... for the breach of the law against lyinge." It does not say what he lied about. (Wouldn't it be interesting if people, e.g. the president of the U.S., were fined for "lyinge"?)

Despite ongoing questions regarding John's arrival and his biological relations, there does appear to be consensus about the nature of John's religious life. From the death of a child to the food on one's plate, religion and faith were visible proofs of one's acceptance and standing in the community throughout the seventeenth century. John was deeply devout in the contexts of Puritan England and America. This is documented in the writings of Westfield Reverend Edward Taylor, who served as minister to John. John's life was characterized by intense spiritual and psychological suffering. Through constant prayer and repentance, he struggled to be what he thought a virtuous man should be, yet his life was forever spent in the shadow of "God's wrath and displeasure."

Let's say John did arrive in America in 1648; employment and a place to stay would have been the order of the day. Previous authors, such as Lillian D. Avery and Charles S. Ripley (both Ingersoll descendants), have indicated that John moved in with Richard Ingersoll, who arrived in 1629 with his family and established a ferry business. Ferries took newly arrived passengers from Beverly to Salem and Boston, Massachusetts. This would be where the skills of immigrant youth were needed for shipbuilding and the expanding housing industry.

Realizing there was little future working on a ferry, I imagine John prayed and pondered his options. He knew bricklaying, but was hesitant to follow the strict rules that permeated the Massachusetts Bay Company and its domineering "oligarchical" leaders, men the likes of John Winthrop, William Bradford and Cotton Mather. A few dozen Commonwealth men oversaw a theocratic society contingent on Puritan church membership. Puritan strictness aside, John continued with his own ritual of daily prayer and religious observance, following the more autonomous Congregationalist church model but under the governance of "Elders."

Hearing of better opportunity in the inland virgin forests, John set off for Hartford, Connecticut in or about 1649, traveling along the "Old Connecticut Path," one of America's earliest westward migration trails that led from Cambridge to Hartford. The trip of 139 miles was made on a two-foot-wide Indian-made trail taking approximately two weeks on foot. The journey, as described by historian James Trumbull, meant trudging over mountains "… through swamps, thickets and rivers. They had no cover but the heavens … The people generally carried their packs, arms and some utensils. …" Stopping at night, they slept in their clothes under the stars in an unprotected, cold wilderness.

Hartford, along with Wethersfield and Windsor, was one of the Three River towns and the beginning of the Connecticut Colony, where land was plentiful and fertile along the Connecticut River. The Massachusetts Bay Company allowed fifty acres per family and fifty for each family member. John needed a wife and children in order to garner more land. As luck would have it, John stayed in a tavern in Hartford run by one of the founding families of the city. Upon dining with John, Magistrate John Webster found him to be of "strong character and godly in his talk and aspirations." The goat he owned, considered at the time to be an "asset of importance," provided cheese, milk and wool. Webster introduced John to Dorothy Lord, daughter of Thomas Lord, another first-family founder, proprietor of Hartford, and a successful mill owner.

John was twenty-five in 1651, when he married the twenty-one-year-old Dorothy Lord, a refined English lady, who had lived in affluence and delicacy in London and later Hartford. The young couple lived the first three years of their married life in the senior Lord's home in Hartford, where Dorothy gave birth to two daughters. Settled in 1636 by the Reverend Hooker and his loyal group of followers, Hartford was an established and flourishing town by 1654.

This same year, Dorothy, a stranger to fatigue and danger, agreed to leave the comfort of her father's home. With John and their two daughters they traveled up the Connecticut River in flat boats to plant the settlement of Northampton. I can only assume that John wanted to strike out on his own, out from under the yoke of his father-in-law, and was persuaded to join the twenty-one planters immigrating up the Connecticut River.

In this rugged frontier outpost, Dorothy gave John a third daughter, dying in childbirth during her delivery. She "spent her last days in constant prayer preparing herself for death." In John's published "relation," a word used by Puritans to describe a public admission of faith, he writes how devastated he felt. He thought that God was playing a trick on him, testing him to see how strong his faith was. A pious church attendee in London, Boston and Hartford, I can imagine John recalling the sermons of the staunch Puritan preacher Thomas Hooker, who moralized that God sent tragedies as a way to correct weakness, "... theirs was not to question God when He took their children or wives."

John's anguish is again well expressed in the following quote from his recorded relation: "... Mr. Mather's ministry was like daggers in my heart. For when I was laboring to hold on to Christ, as I thot, by Faith, it did so rip up my state in such a way as dashed my hopes, whereby, me thot, I was one that went about to establish mine own righteous ... I prayed, searched the scriptures, and attended all duties; but could find no way to get a pardon, of sin, & peace with God, but by repentance of all sin, & a closing with Jesus Christ in faith."

It was a requirement for church membership in the Massachusetts Bay Colony to make a public relation of religious experience. The moral urgings of ministers Hooker, Mather and later Hooker's successor, Samuel Stone, plagued John. His public relation can be found in the unpublished writings of Westfield minister and poet Edward Taylor. This document survives today and can be located in its entirety in libraries as well as the New England Genealogical and Historical Society's Register journal publication, titled The English Origin and Spiritual Turmoil of John Ingersoll. It examines the huge influence of puritan moral and religious teachings that was the bedrock of John's thinking and how he tried to conduct his life. Only with a devout life of prayer and hard work could a person claim salvation within the Puritan value system.

John set about to build his one-room log cabin south of present day Main and Gothic streets in Northampton, Massachusetts. The original settlers negotiated in July 1657 with the local Nonotuck Indian chiefs, through an interpreter, to purchase Northampton for thirty-six shillings, which was later renegotiated and raised to fifty shillings. These white men regarded the Indians as "pagans" but "… purchased the land honestly and paid for it."

However, the Nonotucks had no knowledge of a deed, or the Englishman's language or their concept of ownership, but agreed to accept the fifty shillings to bind the bargain, continuing to have the right to occupy and hunt the land as they had before. These land transfer agreements can be found in the Northampton Town records and are described by historian Charles E. Banks in Volume II of his book, The Planters of the Commonwealth. The English considered the Nonotucks to be of "good disposition," and the two groups, although culturally diverse, lived peacefully for nearly two decades.

The Indians showed the English the practice of annual burning of the forest underbrush, which provided paths – a practice continued for nearly one hundred years. The Nonotucks taught the settlers how to plant, harvest and cook native crops. They explained the many uses of corn, demonstrating the pounding of corn in mortars, a practice the English followed until a mill was constructed in 1659. In addition, the Nonotucks showed the settlers how to carve dugout canoes, how to make and use snowshoes, sew moccasins and how to make warm winter clothing. Lastly, the Natives provided the labor and hunting skills for the lucrative beaver trade until the European demand declined in the next century.

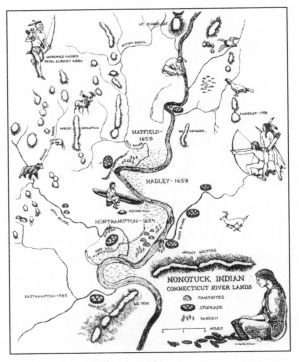

Connecticut River Indian lands: mid-1600's

By 1661, the Northampton settlement had a population of three hundred people. The town built its first church and hired its first permanent minister, Harvard-educated Reverend Eleazer Mather. These early, small groups of Northampton settlers were drawn to the tillable land and initially experienced ease of trade and co-existence with the Indians. The meadowlands were rich and the Connecticut River had an endless bounty of the sea for all to share.

Every man and woman was a farmer, every house was made of logs, every tool was made of wood and every home had a spinning wheel. Beds, tables and chairs were of their own crude workmanship, filling their dark, dank, one-room houses, where a single fireplace burned fifteen to twenty cords of wood a winter. They grew their own food and hunted game in the forests. They ate three coarse, but nutritious meals a day in pewter and wood bowls, with spoons and their fingers. Beer was the common beverage, homemade, until the introduction of apple trees when apple cider took its place. They went to church, prayed regularly, believed in God and were afraid of Satan. Life was hard but sustainable.

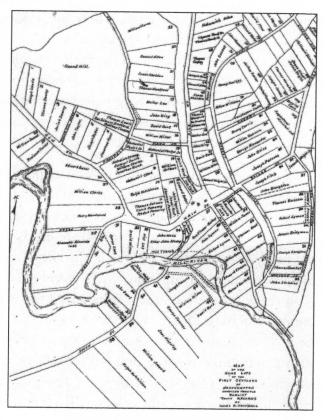

Northampton early settlement

John and his fellow "freemen" all took the Oath of Fidelity to the general government and its overriding jurisdiction in Boston and the English Crown. They ran their local town meetings and governed very much like the towns they left in England. The church was the most important factor in town development, paramount in all things spiritual and political. Matters such as lying, slander, the wearing of silk in a "flaunting manner," missing a town meeting and defamation of character were considered sins and treated with fines and often harsher fees for repeat offenders. These Connecticut River settlements were organized, well run, and governed by the Bay Company's appointee William Pynchon for nearly a half a century.

After Dorothy Lord died in January 1656, John remained in Northampton with his three daughters. His father-in-law offered to help John by arranging an introduction to the Bascom family. Thomas Bascom had arrived in 1634 and was an original settler in the Town of Windsor, and later Northampton. A commissioner and important figure in the new settlement, he advised John to have a new, strong wife – someone who shared his religious vision.

Women of early New England worked as hard as their husbands, farming, brewing, gardening, candle-making, childbearing, nursing, cooking and spinning. The women had to have energy, strength, endurance and character. Abigail Bascom met these requirements and married John in September 1657, eight months after Dorothy had died. Abigail was seventeen when she married John, the common age for marriage in the seventeenth century. The couple lived twelve years in Northampton, acquiring a home with four acres and an additional twenty-three acres of meadow land, earning title and "freeman" designation. (Being a freeman was the property qualification required to have the right to vote in town meetings and acquire more land.) During their life in Northampton, the couple added four daughters to the existing three.

In 1666, for reasons I have not discerned, John, fifty-one, left Northampton with Abigail and his seven daughters and went to nearby Woronoco, "the country of windings," referred to by its English name Westfield. In 1660, Westfield was the western-most settlement of the colony. Other founding families from Northampton and Springfield joined John and Mary, including the Phelps, Cook, Cornish, Dewey, Holyoke, Ponder, Moseley, Root, Noble and Ashley lines. For nearly eleven years these ten families settled into this frontier town in the wilderness with the Hudson River to the west and Canada to the north, in a branch of the Connecticut River valley that rested at the foothills of the Berkshire Mountains. They built the fort where the women and children would "…retire when the men were taking care of the Indians," as told to Lillian Avery. These determined religious men and women cleared the land and transformed it into farms.

The early settlers and Wampanoag Indians inhabited and shared a lush valley of cultivated meadows, where rivers and streams were filled with bass, salmon and shad, and forests were thick with bear, deer and elk. However, the early pioneers frequently suffered intense hardships along the banks of the "little river" that often froze and, along with crop failures, they were often forced to eat acorns for food, except for the maize and succor the Indians gave them. The Indians were generous and amicable with the settlers. These original settlers treated their native hosts honorably. The courage and fortitude of these pioneers had its limits. It did not prevent women from the perils of childbirth. Because there was a lack of proper medical procedures and sanitation, many women's lives were lost in childbirth. Abigail died seven months after the birth of her fourth child, Hester, in 1666, at age twenty-six, the same age Dorothy Lord was when she died.

Following Abigail's death, John was again devastated and bereft. Did he think God was punishing him for not being sufficiently pious and devout? Perhaps God's grace finally shone on John when a year after Abigail died, he met and married Mary Webster Hunt. She took on John's seven children and birthed another eight bringing the total number of children to fifteen.

Mary's father was John Hunt and her mother was Mary Webster, a descendent of Noah Webster of Webster's Dictionary. She was the granddaughter of John Webster, the fifth governor of the Connecticut Colony and a founder of Hartford. It was John Webster who had spotted John in Hartford years before and introduced him to his first wife, Dorothy Lord. Mary Hunt would prove to be an able partner and John's longest living spouse.

John was one of the founders of the first Congregational Church and was referred to by historian Charles Taylor as "one of the Seven Pillars of the Church of Westfield."

The church in these early Connecticut River settlements served both as a meeting house and place of worship, and, without irony, the tavern served as the other place where discussions of all subjects took place. The homes and dwellings of the settlers were clustered near the church building, creating a close-knit community.

Westfield Town records show John was first granted land in 1666 and received an additional grant of twenty acres in 1669. Land grants were given to new settlers and confirmed when improvement of the land continued for five years, all under the supervision of the Hampden district selectmen. The land granted to John Ingersoll and that on which he built his house remained in the Ingersoll family through the nineteenth century and has been referred to as "Ingersoll Place" on the Little River Street, south of the road to Springfield.

Land agreements show that the early settlements in the Connecticut River valley (from Hartford to Westfield) "… were based on humane policy... the land was secured by purchase from the Indians." Hampshire County records show formal purchase of the lands and the conveyance of deeds and title. However, these records are from the point of view of the English and the settlers. As years would show, the "humane" policies were turned on their heads. There are books written about the Native people, from their point of view, some of which I have listed in the bibliography.

With the waning of the beaver trade, plague and the need for grazing and farmland by the settlers, the Indians continued to lose their land. In addition, many tribes could not, or would not adapt to what the Europeans thought was civilized and Christian, "a cotton shirt and baptism," and the ability and willingness to read the Bible.

The early state of affairs between the early settlers and the Wampanoag Indians came to an abrupt end in 1675 with King Philip's War. With the outbreak of hostilities, the authorities in Boston ordered the smaller outlying settlements to move to forted towns. The Westfield townspeople objected to leaving their homes and stayed to fight the Indians, taking refuge in John's "forted" house. The initial cooperation between settlers and Indians deteriorated with the slow but mushrooming growth of the settlements and continued encroachment on Indian land. Many English tried to broker peace during the sporadic and reoccurring inter-tribal Indian wars. One of the most powerful tribes, who reacted to their land being taken, were the Pocumtucks of Deerfield. Many settlers lived in daily fear and confusion, never knowing when individual Natives or bands of three or four would sneak up on their men in the fields or the women in the garden and do them harm, burning their barns, kidnapping or shooting them.

Injustices and disagreements between both the settlers and Indians were addressed under English law, which had little relevance for the

Native peoples. The conflicts between western "civilization" and Indian "savage" culture intensified between 1653 and 1675, igniting the anger of the Wampanoag intertribal leader and sachem Metacomet, known also by his adopted English name of King Philip. The war lasted fourteen months, resulting in brutality on both sides, destroying twelve frontier towns. King Philip's War was the last major effort by the Native peoples to drive out the English settlers. This white man's land-grab system would have repercussions for America's indigenous population for the next four hundred years.

Tragedy and sadness followed John's life and that of his family. His daughter Hester had been captured by Nipmuck Indians and taken to Canada. Hester's first husband, William Gurley, drowned in the Connecticut River when he was twenty-two. Hester then married Benoni Jones and settled in Northampton. Living near the north end of Ft. Tom in Northampton, "...the family of thirty-three persons in the only fortified house were attacked by Indians... nineteen were killed, three escaped, eight were rescued and three carried off." Hester's husband and two young sons, aged four and fourteen months, were killed. Hester was kidnapped and forced to march by foot to Canada. Worn down by exhaustion and the loss of her family, Hester finally succumbed to the "torment" induced by the French priests, trying to convert her to Catholicism, and died in Canada.

John lived out his last years in Westfield, dying in 1684 at age fifty-eight. His youngest child, Jonathan, was only three years old. Mary died six years later in 1690 at age fifty. Town records show they were both buried in Westfield, but their headstones are missing as I found when I visited the Mechanic Street Cemetery.

When I went to search of the Ingersoll homestead and gravestones in Westfield during my visit in 2012, I found a 7-Eleven convenience store, a gas storage facility, sadly neglected houses and a river bank strewn with garbage. In the midst of this stood a historic jewel, alone and resolute, the well-preserved 1723 Dewey House, John Ingersoll's next door neighbor. Walking through the small, dark, twenty- by twenty-foot, one-and-a-half-story red house, I couldn't help but imagine my first generation grandmother, Mary Hunt Webster (ten generations removed), returning to another dark house, without heat except for a low burning fire, at the end of a cold day, to perhaps find a younger daughter mending clothes by candlelight, while another prepared a meal for the youngest children, doing so without running water. Mary may have just returned from Great Barrington where she might have visited a sick grandchild. She would have traveled by horseback in the company of a son, a full day's trip and back.

As I leave this first generation of frontier ancestors, I have two general thoughts about the period in which John and his peers found themselves. First, they had the qualities of self-reliance, dogged determinism, exceptional vigor, religious fervor and the desire for adventure. It seems to me they came for economic reasons, as well as to be free of religious cohesion, which, it turned out, were carried to America where there was a constantly shifting environment of ongoing violence. Seeking God and property were mutually reinforcing.

Secondly, I've gained an increased understanding of the white man's (European and settlers) flaws. Principally, that the settlers looked with ignorance at the Indian's culture and way of life. The settlers saw Indian society through the eyes of European religious institutions and European ways, allowing John and his peers to pursue their acquisition of land through settler colonization.

Their thinking was rooted in the well-established Right of Conquest or the Doctrine of Discovery, the concept of which goes back to the Crusades and Pope Urban II's Papal Bull giving the kings and princes of Europe the right to "discover" or claim land in non-Christian areas in order to build a strong Christian empire. This included the killing and destroying of non-Christian peoples. This practice or system of acquiring wealth by conquest, land-grabbing, destruction, dispossession and killing was not invented by the Europeans; its roots reach back to the Romans and Ottomans but were embedded in the belief system of the European settlers.

In completing this chapter I have tried to understand the past while weighing the history of the "then" against the knowledge I have of "now." The old world order of the laws of conquest were exchanged in the modern world for laws and policies of war. I'm left with more questions than answers. John Ingersoll and my ancestors were among the hundred and fifty thousand settlers who left Great Britain to colonize America in the seventeenth century. By the first federal census of 1790, the young nation had a population of four million Europeans. The Native population had been decimated by nearly seventy-five percent.

CHAPTER 2

SECOND GENERATION
Western Massachusetts

Thomas Ingersoll 1668-1732
Sarah Ashley 1673-1704

*Thomas & Sarah Ingersoll's gravestone
Old Burial Ground, Westfield, Massachusetts*

CHILDREN OF THOMAS & SARAH INGERSOLL

Thomas Ingersoll (1692-1748)
Moses Ingersoll   (1694-1751)
Meriam Ingersoll (1697-1726)
David Ingersoll   (1699-1773)
Eleanor Ingersoll (1704-1732)

Thomas and Sarah Ingersoll

The first boy after John Ingersoll's previous seven daughters, Thomas Ingersoll was born a year after his father married Mary Hunt Webster in 1667, in Westfield, Massachusetts. Mary Hunt then had another seven children with John Ingersoll.

Standing in front of the dirty and lopsided sandstone grave marker for Thomas and his wife Sarah Ashley during my 2012 visit, I wanted to scrub the stone clean. Covered in years of coal dust from an adjacent and now closed coal storage facility, the lettering was barely legible. I imagine Thomas and Sarah's lives in the late 1600's surrounded by rich upland meadows, forests of pine and oak, elk and deer, and the fish-filled Little River (now called the Westfield River, a tributary of the Connecticut River).

Thomas was seven when the King Philip's War broke out, his father an aging frontiersman who witnessed the decimation of the western settlements in Connecticut and Massachusetts. Both Westfield and Springfield were partially burned to the ground on October 5, 1675, including many mills, leaving the towns barely habitable. The Ingersoll family, along with their neighbors, crowded into the Ingersoll's "forted" house during much of the war. (A forted house was a garrison house or a group of houses, built of timbered oak, clustered together inside a stockade fence, eight to ten feet high).

It took almost a half century for burned and pillaged frontier towns to recover after the Indian wars, including King Philip's (1675-1676) and Queen Anne's War (1702-1713). The wars were the result of the ongoing European control of what was called the "New World." The Native people were pushed off and moved farther away from their hunting grounds, rivers and streams. The white man's relentless land expansion, concurrent Indian wars and disease would mark the long path of America's indigenous people's removal and colonization.

Thomas and his wife Sarah would rebuild their home with rifles slung over their shoulders and crosses hung around their necks, facing constant threats of massacre and fire. This second generation couple carried their parent's frontier determinism – they farmed their land and believed salvation was preordained, while fending off the dangers of the wilderness through bravery, faith and trust in the Lord. In their dark, dank twenty- by twenty-one-room log cabin, women cooked, sewed, brewed, made soap and spun clothes, while in the fading evening light, husbands and sons shaved shingles and fashioned wooden farm tools. All this in the midst of subsistence farm life, where they tilled, planted and harvested.

While reshaping the world of America's First People, the Ingersoll family and their English pioneer peers fostered growing democratic institutions, establishing representative governments, with town meetings attended by all freemen. (Free. Men.) Besides farming, other rural occupations – cattle raising, lumbering, dairying, blacksmithing, mill construction, riverside boat building and commerce – were growing.

Like his father, Thomas would have three wives; Sarah Ashley was the first and the mother of his five children. Sarah was one of seventeen children born to her Westfield parents David Ashley and Hannah Glover. She was nineteen when she married Thomas, twenty-four. Common for the time, marriage was a business transaction and likely arranged. As first son, Thomas was heir to his father's property and, in 1692, he and Sarah made their home in his family's inherited house. Thomas would remain there all his life. Sarah would die at age thirty giving birth to her fifth child. Their oldest son, Thomas Jr., would also inherit his father's home and enlarge it.

Sarah Ashley was from a wealthy, slave-owning Springfield family. Fourteen miles east of Westfield, Springfield, the name the English gave the Agwam, was settled in 1636 by Puritan William Pynchon. The Connecticut River town was settled by families including Sarah's great-grandparents Robert Ashley and Mary Eddy Horton Ashley in 1638. In 1661, Sarah's father, Capt. David Ashley, had been one of the original grantees of thirty acres in Westfield. He was an Ingersoll neighbor and a prominent manager of Westfield civic and military affairs. It was David who had written to the government in Boston in 1676 conveying that the inhabitants of Westfield would not abandon their town during King Philip's War.

Sarah's younger brother, Capt. John Ashley, who lived to be ninety, had a son, Col. John Ashley, who became the wealthiest man in Berkshire County. John Ashley would make history when Mumbet, his "servant" whom he renamed Elizabeth Freeman, became the first African enslaved woman to be set free by her own efforts. In 1781, under the Massachusetts State Constitution. Elizabeth Mumbet Freeman was represented by Stockbridge judge and congressman, Theodore Sedgewick.

According to researcher Joseph Carvalha III and annotated in Hampden County, Massachusetts: Black Families in Hampden County, 1650-1965, Sarah and Thomas Ingersoll are listed as owning one slave named Linias. "It was not uncommon for white settlers to own one black slave." according to Carvalha, who goes on to explain that "slaves, free blacks and black indentured servants lived in the communities…" In addition to serving in well-to-do households, it would be common for Westfield townspeople to see slaves hauling water, "boxing" pine trees for turpentine and working in farmers' fields. Service in the military was the primary route to freedom, with owners often granting freedom to their slaves in their wills.

Historian James Truslow Adams in his book, The Founding of New England, describes slave ownership: "Slavery in…New England was so masked that but a slight difference could be perceived in the condition of slaves and hired servants…The younger slaves not only ate and drank but played with the children…The black women were cooks and nurses, and as such assisted their mistresses…in this state of familiar intercourse, instances of cruelty were uncommon…" But settlers in this era viewed the Africans as servants and slaves and saw them as inferior. They also viewed the Native people as inferior "heathens." The early English ministers and settlers "…felt they could "subdue" the "savageness" of the Indians by converting them to Christianity – stamping out their idolatry."

Author John Sedgewick, a Theodore Sedgewick descendent and author of the era, describes Hannah Ashley (wife of John Ashley) and her frequent and cruel temper outbursts with Mumbet in his book, In My Blood: Six Generations of Madness. In addition, he quotes Henry Dwight (son of Judge Sedgewick) as describing John Ashley as "… the gentlest, most benign of men. Hannah Ashley on the other hand was a shrew."

Mumbet's historic lawsuit was evidently triggered by the unstable Hannah Ashley. After securing her freedom at the conclusion of the lawsuit and being awarded thirty shillings in damages, Mumbet returned to work in Colonel Ashley's household. Despite the fact that she was black and her lawsuit helped end the slave trade in Massachusetts, Mumbet is buried in the Ashley family cemetery plot in Stockbridge. The Ashley house built in 1723 is in Sheffield and listed on the National Register of Historic places. A kiosk there summarizes the story of Mumbet and her lawsuit.

John & Hannah Ashley's Home, Ashley Falls, Massachusetts
"Where Mumbet worked"

Thomas Ingersoll would marry twice after Sarah Ashley died – first to Abigail Blakeman and then Ruth Church, but would sire no more children. He would lose two of his brothers, Joseph and Benjamin, in the Queen Anne's War (the second war in the series of French and Indian wars between France and England). Defeated Indian prisoners were not treated well, often executed in public squares, and many were shipped to the Caribbean as slaves.

According to historian Douglas Edward Leach, "These Indian wars were neither glorious nor humane – both sides on many occasions

violated the concept of mercy." In addition to tragedy and disloca-
tion, the Indian wars produced the first veteran problems in America.
Relief came in the form of exemption from certain taxation, land
grants and the "right" to open a Tavern or "Ordinary." Thomas's son
Moses would open an Ordinary in the nearby Berkshire town of Great
Barrington. The emergence of wider paths through continued use of
horses for transportation, along with river travel, would eventually
lead to better roads, albeit dirt ones, in turn increasing the pace of
settler colonization.

The need for a better road system quickly became a priority, and
the Colonial Governors ordered the construction of The Kings Road
between Boston and New York. Opening in 1670, it was initially used
for riders carrying postal packets on horses. The road would not bene-
fit the settlers in Westfield for years. It would be another one hundred
years before nearby Hadley, Massachusetts could claim to have five
horse-drawn chaises. A chaise was a small, open, two-wheeled car-
riage for one or more persons, drawn by one horse. In his role as a
government magistrate, Thomas would regularly make the one-hun-
dred-mile horseback ride to Boston, bringing back news and gossip.
(A magistrate was a major figure in the Colonial court system. A local
official who dealt with minor crimes and who believed his main goal
was to enforce God's plan. Confession for a defendant's sins was considered the goal.)

Isolated in the most western part of Massachusetts, away from the
rapidly growing coastal towns and cities, the first two generations of
Ingersoll families would continue to live settler-based farming lives.
Thomas, Sarah and their extended Massachusetts family found themselves between the development of a global empire on one hand, and
a series of national Indian wars on the other. At the time, there was
the ongoing struggle for the "New World" among Britain, France and

Spain, the origins of which dated back to the sixteenth century. In turn, the religious orthodoxy of the early Ingersoll generations and their peers, alongside the years of Indian wars, would slowly lead to schisms in the eighteenth century. Ruptures were marked by internal strains, inter-colonial quarrels, additional Indian displacement and conflicts and growing secularism.

I've made the assumption that Thomas and Sarah shared the cultural views of their time: belief in English racial, cultural and religious superiority and the underlying legacy claim of the "Right of Discovery." I'd like to believe they treated their servants and Indian neighbors fairly and justly, particularly as they exchanged signed deeds and trade items for land. But I don't know. Unless you were famous like Theodore Sedgewick and William Pynchon, who left written records, you must work your way through the historical inconsistences and opinions of generations of historians. And the Native people did not read or write. Theirs was an oral tradition based on memory. It remains for a future Ingersoll or Ashley sleuth to discover a document or page in a diary to shed light more specifically on Thomas and Sarah's views and norms of conduct.

Although marriages at the time were arranged, it is clear that Thomas held a fondness for his wife Sarah, the mother of his children, as noted in his will located in the Hampshire County probate files. He refers to her as "My beloved wife Sarah." In addition, they share a joint headstone whose epitaph reads:

"This stone stands but to tell
where their dust lies
not what they was
when saints shall rise
that day will show
what part they acted
here below"

Thomas Ingersoll Family Genealogy
[18th Century original]

CHAPTER 3

THIRD GENERATION

Great Barrington, Massachusetts

Moses Ingersoll 1694-1751
Catherine Tryn Van Slyke & Family 1694-1772

Ingersoll "Troy" Ordinary, Great Barrington, Massachusetts
[Photo circa 1850's]

CHILDREN OF MOSES AND CATHERINE INGERSOLL

Thomas Ingersoll	(1720-1742)
Eleanor Ingersoll	(1722-1772)
Joanna Ingersoll	(1726-1783)
Lydia Ingersoll	(1727-1804)
Elizabeth	(1729-1793)
Peter Ingersoll	(1733-1785)
David Ingersoll	(1736-)
Bathsheba Ingersoll	(1738-1800)

Moses Ingersoll

Moses was the second son of Thomas Ingersoll and Sarah Ashley. He was born sixteen years after the end of the King Philip's War, when the greater Springfield-Westfield area was still recovering from the devastation of its settlements. Both his grandparents, the original settlers John and Mary Ingersoll were deceased by the time he was born. However, there were siblings, cousins, nieces and uncles all nearby. He had two brothers, Thomas who remained in Westfield, and David who settled in Great Barrington, and two sisters, Eleanor and Meriam, both of whom died in their twenties.

As he grew older, Moses, like many of his Westfield folk, had the opportunity to travel and broaden his horizons along the New England Fur Trail that wound through Kinderhook, New York, a much larger and established Dutch community. Moses met and courted his wife Catherine Tryn Van Slyke while visiting Kinderhook. They were both twenty-five when they married in Westfield in 1719. The couple would have eight children and eventually settle in Great Barrington.

Most of the sons, daughters and married Ingersoll grandchildren would remain in Westfield, but being a second-born son meant Moses was not entitled to his father's land. He and Catherine resided for a while at his mother's Ashley family farm and home in nearby Springfield. The couple would leave the Westfield-Springfield area along with Moses' brother David and become early settlers in Sheffield – only to then re-settle in Great Barrington in 1726.

I admit I think of Arlo Guthrie and his song "Alice's Restaurant" when Great Barrington is mentioned. But in the eighteenth century this Berkshire countryside was a wilderness of forests, streams and the mighty Housatonic River. Moses developed his own land passion, which carried him sixty miles west, from the Westfield, Springfield and the Connecticut River valley to the Housatonic River and the Berkshire Mountains.

Moses would establish an Ordinary, the original Massachusetts term used for a tavern, in Great Barrington. In her book, Stage Coach and Tavern Days, historian Alice Earl states that in 1656 the General Court in Boston ordered "one sufficient inhabitant" of each town to keep an Ordinary. For weary travelers on the early narrow trails and for the local town people, the Ordinary was a place of libation, rest, camaraderie and news. By the warmth of the fire in the tavern parlor, Moses and Catherine would have served the popular flip, a drink made in a pewter mug or earthen pitcher filled with two thirds strong beer, sweetened with molasses or dried pumpkin and flavored with a dash of gill, a New England rum. Into this mixture was thrust a red-hot loggerhead. "This was often followed by a meal served in a trencher, a wooden or metal plate full of stewed meat, codfish or pumpkin and after the meal, a shared bed in a cold upstairs bed-room. (Actually sounds good, doesn't it? Without the cold bedroom of course.)

Moses became the proprietor of two and a half Rights (four hundred acres in a Right) in Great Barrington, in addition to a thousand acres of land across the street that he eventually purchased. His residence on South Main Street was where his son, Capt. Peter Ingersoll, would build his own house. In his History of Great Barrington, nineteenth-century historian Charles Taylor describes Moses as an innkeeper and "...a large landholder, in comfortable circumstances, a prominent man amongst the settlers, and held office as parish treasurer."

Life was somewhat improved for those of Moses' generation. Although there was no hereditary aristocracy in Colonial America, there were several class distinctions. Being an original settler grantee and having access to additional cheap land, allowed Moses rapid advancement.

By the turn of the century, racial discrimination – originally based on religious views – was easing with the diminishing influence of the original Puritan values and doctrines. But the young Colonial society was still tainted by the remnants of the spiritual crisis of the 1692 Salem Witch Trials. And Jesuit missionaries and Yale-educated ministers were actively trying to save souls by converting the Native River Tribes to Christianity and assimilating the Indians into the cultural ways of the English.

Every family continued to own an imported copy of the Bible, and the leading men and their families would have had other imported religious books of hymns, spiritual songs, catechism, prayers and sermons. The first printing press arrived in Boston in 1640. It was followed by a growing number of small printing offices that published government laws, almanacs, sermons, politically themed letters and blank legal forms.

But Boston remained a coastal city industry. Only with the publication of news sheets such as the Boston News Letter in 1704, did news start to proliferate inland. Prior to the pamphlet, news had been spread by word of mouth and correspondence and dealt with local interests. Moses' father, Thomas, having served in his capacity as magistrate in the Boston General Court, would have been the purveyor of news for his family and neighbors in western Massachusetts.

As this generation of Ingersoll family men enriched themselves, they served in public offices and retained a great deal of power in Berkshire and Hampden counties. Land incrementally purchased from the Indians was granted to English settlers by magistrates and selectmen in Springfield, which governed western Massachusetts under the rules and guidance of the General Court (the legislature) in Boston and ultimately the King of England. America was, after all, a colony of England.

Moses' brother David was one of the chief spokesmen for the establishment of the Parish of Sheffield and instrumental in establishing the town of Great Barrington. In addition to Moses and his family, Great Barrington attracted new settlers from Westfield, Northampton and Springfield in 1725 and 1726. Family members from the original settlement of Westfield (Woronoko), including Dewey, Noble, Root, Phelps and Ashley, moved, wanting to acquire more fertile soil.

Moses' older brother Thomas was an attorney and early surveyor of meadow lands. Like his father before him, Thomas Jr. also served as a magistrate. He was commissioned by George I, twelve times elected selectman in Westfield and served as the district representative at the General Court in Boston. Legend has it that Thomas shot the famous Abenaki military Indian leader Grey Lock while the chief was trying to scalp Mrs. Ingersoll. Grey Lock, born in Westfield, made regular sporadic attacks on the Connecticut River towns between 1723 and 1726 in retaliation for his tribe losing their way of living (fur trade and hunting) and for land lost due to escalating English colonization.

In 1736, along with other prospective landowners, Thomas negotiated with the Mohican Indian River tribe Sachem Konkapot for additional Berkshire acres. Mohican or (Mahican) was the English word for the Berkshire Indians, who were eastern Algonquian Natives, and referred to themselves as Muhhekunneuw. According to Berkshire historian Lion Miles in his book, "A Life of John Konkapot," Chief Konkapot was a "man of prudence...just and upright," a tribal leader who welcomed the settlers, attempting to protect the rights of his people through compromise and signing land deeds with his "turkey foot" totem symbol signature. The Mohicans did not possess the concept of English land ownership or the European acquisition of possessions. They did not possess writing skills, so could not understand English written agreements. Theirs was an oral tradition based on memory, honor and handshake.

The Mohicans and the numerous hosts of independent sub-tribes of western Massachusetts lived in fairly large villages located on top of mounded and fortified Berkshire Hills. Wigwams, consisting of twenty to thirty mid-sized Long Houses, were located near large cornfields. These river tribes were hunter-gatherers who lived according to the seasons. The Berkshire tribes were self-sufficient, self-reliant, had distinct dialects and spoke different languages. Their agriculturally based diet was supplemented by game, fish and a mixed variety of berries and nuts from the forests and valleys. They smoked fish and sun dried food for winter preservation, hunted for winter water fowl. Throughout New England, many tribes were in a state of continuous inter-tribal warfare. However, it was the ever-increasing colonization of Native lands that often unified the tribes to fight the settlers.

Encouraging his people to embrace Christianity, Konkapot learned English and accepted Northampton minister and missionary Jonathan Edwards, allowing him to preach among the river Mohican tribes. Konkapot served as interpreter for several years to Edwards, before Edwards left to become president of Princeton University in 1758. He then translated for Moses' son-in-law, Reverend Samuel Hopkins.

During this time, the General Court in Boston kept creating new towns on Konkapot's eleven thousand acres of tribal land. Konkapot, called Captain Konkapot by the English, served as the first selectman of Stockbridge. He attended most town meetings, served in multiple town offices and was often referred to as the founder of Stockbridge. The Mission House, built in approximately 1739, is a major tourist attraction and historical landmark in Stockbridge, depicting the eighteenth-century Berkshire river tribes during the Colonial missionary era. Visiting Stockbridge in the fall of 2017, I was given a tour of the recently restored Mission House by Curator Mark Wilson.

Walking through the furnished rooms, I could imagine the Ingersoll son-in-law Samuel Hopkins sitting by the fire with Jonathan Edwards discussing the complex conversion issues of the river Indians, as Konkapot stood listening.

The Housatonic and Connecticut rivers continued to be a highway of transportation along with the old Indian paths. The early settlers from the Westfield families acquired their initial Berkshire land from the Mohican Indians in consideration of "four hundred and sixty pounds, three barrels of sider and thirty quarts of rum." The district representatives executed a deed conferring land along the Housatonic that included Sheffield, Great Barrington, Mt. Washington, Ergrement and Stockbridge. These same men were empowered by the appointed magistrates and district representatives to admit settlers for an allotted amount of land and to give them the time of three years to bring forward a settlement to "build a suitable house, till the land and reserve enough land for a minister and school for thirty shillings for each one hundred acres."

By 1774, the river tribes had naively conceded several thousand acres through English written agreements and deeds. By 1822, most of the Berkshire Indian tribes moved or were resettled in Wisconsin by order of the U.S. federal government as per federal government policy. This Indian Removal Policy was first envisioned by President Thomas Jefferson, structured by James Monroe and pushed into callous and inhumane law in 1830 by President Andrew Jackson.

Moses' brother David settled in Great Barrington and was "a man of some enterprise," according to Berkshire historian Charles Taylor. He kept a small goods store near the Great Bridge and was one of the earliest merchants of the parish. Moses deeded his land near the river to David, thereby controlling the water power. With the water privilege, David erected a saw mill, grist mill and iron works. The two brothers controlled a great deal of land and industry in Great Barrington. The water power of the Housatonic River alone allowed for improvements in the town, including the grist mill where grain could be turned into flour or meal. The mills later became part of the Dewey Mills and were then occupied by the Berkshire Woolen Company.

But all was not calm for these free-enterprise brothers. Like their parents and grandparents before them, the Ingersoll family and their neighbors were still subject to Indians raids as described by Moses' son-in-law Reverend Samuel Hopkins in his journal dated July 9, 1755: [sic] "Two or three Indians chased a man about a mile and u west of my house. Upon this news we thought it not prudent to live at my house and have therefore concluded to lodge at Mother Ingersoll's this night." Hopkins preached to the sub-tribes of the Mohican, the Housatonic and Stockbridge Indians in Stockbridge, Great Barrington and Sheffield throughout his career. All the while Hopkins witnessed the English taking of Indian lands and the ongoing attempts by several small Indian tribes to fight back.

It was this ceaseless Indian and settler warfare, along with the continued African slave trade, that laid the foundation for the political and economic fabric of the nation.

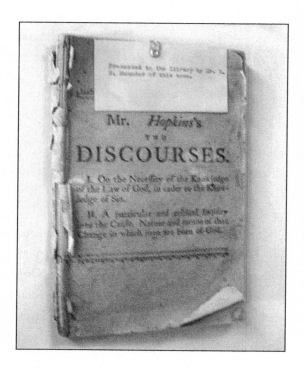

Religious Discourses of Reverend Samuel Hopkins

Catherine Van Slyke Ingersoll

Much of my Ingersoll research focuses on the paternal side of the family, the men. Ferreting out information on Ingersoll women, other than childbirth death information, has been difficult. But I got lucky with Moses' wife, Catherine Tryn Van Slyke. She was a descendent of a Dutch fur trader and Mohawk Indian. I found information that shed some light on racial issues of the early settlers and elaborated on in Thomas N. Ingersoll's book, To Intermix with our White Brothers: Indian Mixed Blood in the U.S. from Earliest Times to the Indian Removal. The book highlights the behavior of the four early European groups, the Spanish, English, Portuguese and French, and the "… exploitation of the Indians, labor and resources, violent conflict with them, and white supremacy marked by racial mixture at the social periphery."

Catherine was the great-granddaughter of a Dutch first setter and fur trader in Schenectady, New York, Cornelius Antonissen Nieffins Van Slyke, and Ots Toch, a Mohawk of the Turtle Clan. Catherine's mother, Johana Hanse Barheit, and father, Pieter Willemse Van Slyke, lived in Kinderhook, New York. Records from the NYBGS (an on-line data base), show Catherine's Dutch great-grandfather in Canada in the early 1600's, trading with and living among the Mohawk Indians. But Catherine's genealogy shows variant records. It is unclear whether Catherine's grandmother, Baertje Nieffens, was the daughter of Ots Toch and Jacque Hertel or Ots Toch and Cornelius Nieffins Van Slyck. Hertel was a French boy of sixteen who was a trader from Normandy and was one of three interpreters for Samuel de Champlain, having arrived with him in Canada in 1613. Was Hertel father or spouse of Ots Toch? I found the detective research work often difficult. But when a discovery is made, a mystery solved, the sleuthing can be thrilling.

In the early 1600's, the Mohawks dominated the fur trade in Quebec and upstate New York, along with the Dutch and French. Both groups married or had unions with Mohawk women. Indians referred to as "Praying Indians" were Indians Christianized by Jesuit missionaries. There was discrimination regarding the children of "half breeds" from the first generation but it dissipated by the third generation. When Moses married Catherine, she was three generations removed from her Mohawk and Dutch ancestors. (For over three centuries the Native people were viewed as heathens, uncivilized and in need of conversion to Christianity.)

As a female in the first half of the eighteenth century, there was little need for a woman to read or write except for the Bible. As a young girl growing up in the Dutch Albany, New York area, Catherine and her siblings would have had occasional catechism lessons by a visiting "voorlezer" – the Dutch word for "reader," a lay person who also conducted hymn singing. However, as recorded in the Hampshire County probate files, Catherine's repeated mark on her husband Moses' Last Will and Testament is a clumsy "X."

In a phone conversation with the current Kinderhook Town Historian, Ruth Piwonka "...a number of people (male and female) of Great Barrington did not read or write very frequently or with great skill. There was little need for it." I will assume Catherine read the bible but could not write. She cared for the children, spun, cooked, helped in the tavern. Her son-in-law, Yale-educated Reverend Samuel Hopkins, was married to her daughter, Joanna, and spent his career fostering Christianity among the Berkshire tribes. He was also an ardent abolitionist. Neighbor and friend Judge Joseph Dwight, chief justice of Berkshire County, oversaw the disposition of Moses' estate, and was for many years a trustee of the Native Indian School in Stockbridge. Surrounded by these progressive men. I infer that

Catherine's status in her Ingersoll family and among her English community was valued for her domestic contributions.

As a family of means, Catherine and Moses most probably had an African servant. Catherine's father, Peter Van Slyke, in his will recorded in 1735, records his leaving "two Negroes" to his son Dirik. Left – meaning they were property and not free? Inter-marriage among white settlers and Native Americans existed and was frequently recorded, but I could find no documents referencing marriage between whites and Africans.

To Moses, land was most important. Land made him a man of means, with a business (tavern) and a place of qualification in his Church, securing his position of "age & estate" in society. His era saw the merchant, lawyer and speculator classes become the favored economic groups, increasing the disparity between rich and poor. In the first half of the century (1713-1745), imported English culture was replaced by a native-born one. In addition, there was the growth of commerce, roads, the press, increasing secularism. There were also ongoing land disputes. The formal introduction of the profession "surveyor" early in the next century would slowly bring change and clarification to contentious land issues.

Moses would die at fifty-seven, but left a will and a large and generous estate for his family. The will can be viewed in the Hampshire County probate file papers in Northampton, located in the online data base of the New England Genealogical Historical Society. Catherine would survive him to the then ripe old age of seventy-eight. She continued to enjoy her family and help her son Peter Ingersoll run the tavern, where plots were spun by the "Sons of Liberty." The secret society regularly met in the tavern to discuss politics – how to protect their rights and how to fight the unfair taxation by the British government.

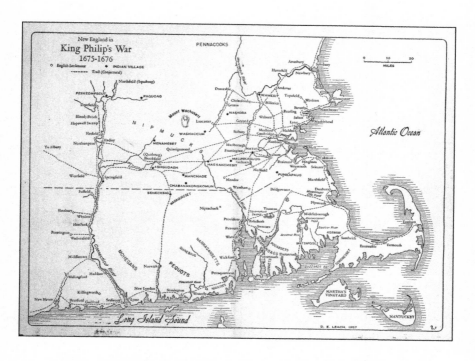

Map of Native American tribes in King Philip's War

CHAPTER 4

FOURTH GENERATION
Great Barrington, Massachusetts

᳐

Captain Peter Ingersoll 1733- 1785
Anna Severill 1731- 1781

Wainwright Inn, Great Barrington, Massachusetts – 2015

CHILDREN OF PETER & ANNA SEVERILL INGERSOLL

Oliver Ingersoll	(1752-1826)
Thomas Ingersoll	(1753-1844)
Moses Ingersoll	(1755- 1834)
Mary Ingersoll	(1757-1784)
Israel Ingersoll	(1765-1790)
Peter Ingersoll	(1765-1834)

Captain Peter Ingersoll

In the fall of 2015, I visited Great Barrington and stayed at the Inn that had been the home of my Patriot ancestors, Peter Ingersoll and his wife Anna Severill. Originally known as the Troy Tavern, the Ingersoll house served as a popular tavern during the Colonial era. It is now the Wainwright Inn and is located on what was the New England Path. An important thoroughfare in western Massachusetts, it ran from Albany to Hartford to Boston. Here in the fertile Berkshire valley, bookended by the Berkshire Mountains and with the Housatonic River running through the heart of the downtown, Peter and Anna raised their six children, ran their tavern and farm, and experienced the American War of Independence.

During my three-day visit, I tried to imagine what my ancestors' lives were like. Staying in their home, I could feel an older, ghost structure beneath its exterior. After ambling through the first floor parlor, library and upstairs bedrooms, I ventured down into the basement. The original brick foundation laid by Peter's father, Moses, seemed fresh. I ran my hand across the massive foundation boulders covered in whitewash paint.

Each night as I lay in the creaky, four-poster bed on the second floor, I imagined rowdy travelers drinking downstairs by the warmth of the fire – "in the parlor ... with fine wallpaper with scenes of a fox chase" as described in a publication of that time. In those days travelers often were assigned to one bed. Strangers who drank together downstairs would sleep together upstairs. I wondered how Peter's and Anna's children rested with all the noise. Did their mother calm them or was she in the tavern refilling the flip crock or serving a seasonal stew?

Did they have servants? Although life for women in the eighteenth century was less severe than in the seventeenth century, women still endured the burden of childbirth; they did the sewing, laundry, candle-making, bandage making and farming. They cooked with copper or brass pots often weighing forty pounds and lifted kettles that held fifteen gallons. Peter grew up helping his father and mother in the tavern and farm.

Housatonic River, Great Barrington, Massachusetts

On my second day, and to get a sense of the place and its river, I decided to walk the River Walk along the Housatonic. The defiant river teems over rocks and boulders, winding and churning as it snakes through the downtown. Dotted with empty and derelict nineteenth century textile and paper mills, the sound of the river drums out all other sounds, particularly automobiles. The river, I was told, was still full of perch, bass and pike. The forests of spruce, hemlock and birch are still full of elk, bear, squirrel and fox. But the Housatonic River Indians are gone.

Life in eighteenth century Massachusetts and New England was marked by a high standard of living for most of the colonists. They enjoyed self-sufficiency, vibrant communities with town governments, church, local newspapers, blacksmiths, tanners, coopers, an abundance of food and the occasional imported luxury from Great Britain. However, slowly this all changed for Peter and his family. As a middle-aged man, Peter would be called up to fight against England's coercive acts and regulations. Like many tavern owners, Peter held secret meetings in the Troy Tavern for the Sons of Liberty, discussing and plotting how to deal with their British overloads.

Precipitated by the arrival of the "lobster-backs" (the term the Patriots called the red-jacketed British soldiers) in Boston in 1768, real planning began. With the closing of the Boston port in 1774, the Massachusetts and New England Patriots slowly garnered the incentive to unite and fight. Taverns were the first public structures, and Massachusetts taverns in the seventeenth century were considered by many to be the incubators of the American Revolution. It was in taverns like the Ingersoll's Troy Tavern where the Sons of Liberty met to drink beer and rum, eat and argue politics and eventually took up their muskets. Writer Susan Cheever in her 2016 book, Drinking America, implies that the defiance and rage against England was fueled by the regular consumption of alcohol.

The reasons the American colonists revolted against Great Britain were many: economic (unfettered and unreasonable tax acts), religious, political and social. But driving the colonists was the fierce desire for self-determination. For more detail, Charles Taylor's History of Great Barrington and Kevin Phillip's 1775: A Good Year for a Revolution are both good sources. The colonists' optimism and willingness to stand against the authority of their mother country was key. The inability of the cash-starved British Empire to put down an insurgency thousands of miles away, after a war lasting seven years, would see an end to British suppression with the signing of the Treaty of Paris in 1783.

Great Barrington was a point of some importance during the Revolution – as a depot for military stores, provisions and supplies for the army. Peter's Troy Tavern was used as a fort and colonial armory during the seven-year revolution. Washington's chief Continental artillery officer, Henry Knox, passed through Great Barrington. Knox was transporting over 120,000 pounds of artillery over three hundred miles of iced rivers, forests and roads with the pure muscle power of his troops. Legend has it that Knox stopped overnight in the Ingersoll Tavern before delivering the artillery that led to the ultimate liberation of the city of Boston.

Peter served in the first campaign of the Revolutionary War as part of the Ninth Regiment in Boston, along with other Great Barrington, Sheffield, Egrement and Stockbridge men. He would see action in four major battles: Bunker Hill, Saratoga, Trenton and Princeton. A list of the company under the command of Captain Ingersoll in 1776 shows it contained 78 men, "… its equipment consisted of 24 guns, 2 bayonets, 6 cartridge boxes, 5 pounds of powder, 4 pounds balls and 6 spare flints." This paucity of equipment is evidence of the scarcity of stores, where every gun and powder spared from home defense was pressed into service.

The Berkshire militia preformed an important service throughout the revolution and was frequently called out for border service and to reinforce the Continental army. The militia system of the state required the enrollment of all men capable of bearing arms. They furnished their own rifles, shot pouch, powder horns, blankets, knapsacks and clothing. The Ninth of Great Barrington included Peter's relatives and neighbors. John Ashley of Sheffield, a brother-in-law through marriage, was a Major General under whom Peter served at the battle of Saratoga; Peter's uncle, Major Thomas Ingersoll, was also part of the Ninth, who, after the war, was accused of being a Loyalist. It was not uncommon for Loyalists and Patriots to change sides during the eight-year war. Even Benjamin Franklin was a Loyalist before switching over to the Patriot cause. (A Loyalist was a British supporter.)

The era that encompassed Peter's lifetime not only included the War of Independence but the growing diminishment of Jeffersonian Republicanism and the ascendency of Adams and Hamilton Federalism, well-chronicled as an outcome of the national expansion of publishing, pamphlets, newsletters and newspapers of colonists' ideas.

I wonder if the writings of Mercy Otis Warren, the Muse of the Revolution and an early activist, and other emerging authors, including Mary Wollstonecraft's Vindication of the Rights of Women, influenced Colonial wives and mothers. The settler family of this era was better educated. Education and culture, organized in the home, centered on reading – the Bible for women, the classics for men, and history in the upper-end households. Civics and culture were male, and household and domestic responsibilities were for women.

What did they think of slavery? Or the diminished Mohican tribe, which had been relocated to central New York along with the other Housatonic River Tribes? By 1774, and after the American

Revolution, the River Tribes had naively conceded several thousand acres in English-written agreements and deeds. By 1822, most of the remaining Berkshire tribes moved or were resettled in Wisconsin by order of the U.S. Government. This Indian Removal Policy was first envisioned by President Thomas Jefferson, structured by James Monroe and pushed into callous and inhuman law in 1830 by President Andrew Johnson.

The Treaty of Paris brought an end to the eight-year War of Independence, but its aftermath also brought a new state constitution and government, as well as wide-scale corruption. Several Boston oligarchs tried to enrich themselves at the expense of the many. War debt and bankruptcies were everywhere, and the patriot farmers were the main victims, many going to debtor's prison. Poll and land taxes (head-count tax and wealth tax) on farmers' depreciated properties were boosted to pay down the state war debt, and Massachusetts had one of the largest. The unresolved grievances would result in the Springfield Armory Uprising in 1786. Called Shays' Rebellion, it would force George Washington out of retirement.

Although Peter died prior to Shays' Rebellion, his sons and several of his nephews and cousins in western Massachusetts would join the aggrieved farmers. The war debt and the state's reduced economic circumstances would set in motion the immigration of the younger Ingersoll men and women to less expensive lands, less debt and less restrictive governments.

Peter would remain in his home until the time of his death in 1785, with an unproven blemish on his reputation. A court martial, according to a diary entry by Lt. Gamaliel Whiting of Great Barrington, cited in Charles Taylor's History of Great Barrington, read, "Dec. 4. Peter Ingersoll try'd by Court Marsh'll." A more detailed account by diarist Samuel Bixby states: "Capt. Ingersoll was tried by a Court

Martial for spreading false reports ... tending to defame the General ... (Washington). He was fined 8 shillings ..." Are these diaries reliable? I could find no official military record of a court martial.

Anna had died before Peter. Their burial marker is inscribed "Mount Peter" and is reported to be on top of the mounded hill across the street from the family manse, overlooking the Housatonic River. The hill was too steep, slippery and overgrown for me to climb to look for the burial site. Nor could I find a copy of the probate file for Peter, which is odd as Peter's father left a large estate and a lengthy recorded will. (Peter is one of my Daughters of the American Revolution Patriots. Because the DAR is a lineage-based organization, you must document your lineage to a person or persons who fought in America's War of Independence.)

The next generation of Ingersolls would leave the Berkshires, traveling west along the Mohawk Indian Trail through Albany and across New York State to Onondaga County in upstate New York, south of Lake Ontario. Gone with the migrating Ingersolls were most of the Mohican and River Indians, leaving only the Mahaiwe Preforming Arts Center – the Mohican name for the area, meaning "the place downstream."

CHAPTER 5

FIFTH GENERATION
Liverpool, New York

Thomas Ingersoll 1753-1843
Hannah Joyner 1767-1844

Grave Monument for Thomas and Hannah Ingersoll
Liverpool Cemetery, New York

CHILDREN OF THOMAS INGERSOLL AND HANNAH JOYNER

Peter Ingersoll	(1785-1863)
Cornelius Ingersoll	(1787-1863)
Hannah Ingersoll	(1790-1846)
Lucy Ingersoll	(1795-1858)
Caleb Joyner Ingersoll	(1800-1893)
Panthus Ingersoll	(1802-1876)
Betsy Ingersoll	(1805-1886)
Evelena Ingersoll	(1807-)

CHILDREN OF THOMAS INGERSOLL AND LYDIA DEWEY INGERSOLL

David Ingersoll	(1773-1842)
Thomas Ingersoll	(1775-1847)
Laura Ingersoll	(1775-1868)
Ann Ingersoll	(1777-)
Joseph Dwight	(1778- 1861)
Hiram Ingersoll	(1780-1865)
Ann Ingersoll	(1782-1846)
Lydia Ingersoll	(1784-)

Original Deed Transfer Record, Office of Registry,
Great Barrington, MA

Thomas Ingersoll

M y voyage of discovery continued with Thomas Ingersoll, the first-born son and one of six children of Peter Ingersoll and Anna Severill of Great Barrington, Massachusetts. I knew he served briefly, a total of nineteen days, with the Berkshire Militia Regiment in the War of Independence. He would see the end of the Revolution but also its consequences: a doubling of the Massachusetts debt, Congress churning out paper money, the failure of Massachusetts to create a domestic industry (after years of a trade-based economy with England), bankrupt farmers, and a post-war depression. I returned to Great Barrington in the fall of 2017 to flush out more information.

Debt saddled, hounded by creditors and unable to pay old family war debts and new taxes, Thomas decided to leave western Massachusetts. Together with three of his brothers and their families, Thomas left the area in 1785, shortly after his father died, and

immigrated west to New York. Only one brother and sister remained
in Massachusetts, both died in their mid-twenties with no recorded
spouses or children. It is also likely that Thomas and his brothers were
affected by the so-called court martial of their father, Captain Peter
Ingersoll, "… for spreading false reports about the Country, tending
to defame the General (Washington)…" The family reputation was
damaged.

Why was Thomas eager to stake out his own land and future when,
as the oldest son he was entitled to his father's property? I was curious.
I spent two hours in the Great Barrington Office of Registry. Among
the stacks of plastic-wrapped eighteenth-century ledger books, I care-
fully turned brittle parchment pages of deeds until I found Thomas's
name. Inked in neat brown script, written by quill pen, were multiple
transfer citations. Then, the record of the last transfer of the Ingersoll
home on Main Street to David Wainwright in 1790 for three hundred
pounds. Thomas was referred to as "Yoeman," stating his residence as
Chinangoo, Montgomery County, New York. It took five years to
convey clear title to David Wainwright.

Partial Deed Image, Great Barrington, MA

Thomas would begin anew. After burying his first wife, Lydia Dewey, in 1784, Thomas took a second wife, Hannah Joyner, aged seventeen. With his new wife and the eight children he had with Lydia Dewey, Thomas left western Massachusetts, traveling across New York State along the Mohawk Trail, also called the Great Indian or Iroquois Trail, which connected Albany to Fort Oswego on Lake Ontario. As a Revolutionary War veteran, Thomas probably journeyed in a caravan with other veterans, friends and families. In lieu of cash for returning soldiers, the bankrupt government gave veterans land grants, sparking the greatest migration outside New England states to New York, Pennsylvania and Ohio. Massachusetts had the largest war debt, $14,000,000, including $900,000 owed to veterans.

These New England settlers heard the best soil and title lay west. Thomas and Hannah took with them improved methods of agriculture, enterprise, ingenuity and social habits. The family, with all their belongings, rode wagons through glutinous black mud and deeply rutted dirt roads, making their home finally in Liverpool, a small lakeside town on Lake Onondaga, a few miles north of Syracuse. This had been Onondaga territory, one of the five nations of the Iroquois, many of whom moved to Canada with land grants given by Great Britain for their having sided with the British during the war.

Thomas and Hannah Joyner would have eight more children, adding to the eight that Thomas was already father to. Like many struggling settler farmers, Thomas could not afford servants or slaves and relied for labor on his own abundant supply of children, giving additional insight into the reason for the large colonial families, necessary, in part, for their own food production. By age ten, boys worked in the fields with their fathers while girls assisted their mothers in the house and garden.

Liverpool, known to have excellent soil, soon became a busy boat community and, when incorporated in 1830, five years after the opening of the Erie Canal, the town supported a large boat-repair industry as well as a large salt-producing industry. Thomas and his family remained in Liverpool for sixty years. He lived to ninety, his wife Hannah to seventy-seven, dying within a year of her husband.

At the time of their deaths in the 1840's, the colonies had been absorbed into a country whose borders extended from coast to coast. Their children would scatter, pulled by stories of good land. Only seven of the sixteen children would remain in Liverpool, and their oldest son Caleb (in my line) would leave New York and immigrate to Michigan. Most early American agrarian families had a dozen or more children. Due to the complexity of the many children and marriages, I have kept this Ingersoll narrative to my direct line, and, over the past seven years, visited every town where they lived. Thomas is the exception. I know the least about him and make assumptions about why he left Great Barrington.

Thomas and Hannah, as well as many of their Liverpool offspring, are buried in the Liverpool Town Cemetery. Their monument spells the name with two ll's – Ingersoll. Throughout most of the eighteenth and seventeenth centuries, the name on Massachusetts Town and Vital Records is spelled as Ingersole. Most censuses I examined had multiple and inconsistent spellings. The original English spelling as found in St. Warburg's Church in Derby, England, records the name spelled Inkersall.

CHAPTER 6

Sixth Generation
New York & Michigan

Caleb Joyner Ingersoll 1800-1992
Celinda Carey 1805-1868

Ingersoll Family Monument
Three Oaks Cemetery, Buchanan, Michigan

CHILDREN OF CALEB JOYNER INGERSOLL & CELINDA CAREY

Martha Ingersoll	(1826-1895)
Maloan Ingersoll	(1830-1895)
Maria Ingersoll	(1833-1878)
Mantha Ingersoll	(1835-1916)
Maranda Ingersoll	(1838-1909)
Monroe Ingersoll	(1852-1913)
Celinda Ingersoll	(1852-1857)

Caleb Joyner (CJ) Ingersoll

Caleb was the fifth child of Thomas and Hannah Joyner Ingersoll, the tenth of sixteen children from his father's two marriages. He was born in 1800 in Onondaga County, New York, four years prior to the Lewis and Clark Expedition and President John Adams residency in Washington, D.C. He was seven when Robert Fulton's Claremont went up the Hudson River in 1807, marking the beginning of steam technology. Steam-powered ships would capture Caleb's imagination and lead him to a life on the sea in addition to farming.

When he was twelve Caleb left home, which wasn't unusual in those days, to work as a cabin boy on a schooner on Lake Ontario. During the War of 1812 between Great Britain and Colonial America, Caleb's ship was sunk and burned, and the crew of his ship captured by the British. In her genealogy of the Ingersoll family, Lillian Avery wrote that Caleb "...after being held prisoner for three months in an old hulk, was released and walked to his home."-

In 1819, at age nineteen, known as "C J" Ingersoll, and while still living in New York, Caleb joined the Masons. The Masons (or Freemasons) date back to fifteenth-century European stoneworker fraternities. The quasi-religious, secret, male-only society mushroomed in America during the eighteenth and nineteenth centuries. The society became known as the Odd Fellow and Masonic Lodges, with the emphasis on performing good works and becoming a "better man." Four presidents were Masons: George Washington, James Monroe, Franklin D. Roosevelt and Harry Truman.

Did this organization make Caleb a better man? I don't know. But in his January 20, 1892 obituary in the Niles Weekly Mirror, Caleb was described as having "...brought many a man from darkness to 'more light'...and was "known to be a most worthy and exemplary member of the order." Did the Masons idea of a better man mean a civilized man – a Bible-instructed male Christian (preferably white), able to read, write, work and wear proper clothes? I don't know.

Caleb was a charter member of the St. Joseph Valley Lodge, No. 4, the oldest in Michigan. He helped found Buchanan Lodge, No. 68 in 1843, serving as a Masonic "Master" for many years. When I called and spoke with the curator of the Masonic Lodge in Buchanan last year, he kindly sent me a photo of Caleb's silver-headed cane handle with its Masonic emblem and plaque, which remains in the Buchanan Mason Lodge Museum today. When I asked about research and access to minutes and papers of the local lodge, I was politely told that was not possible.

Cane Handle Inscribed CJ, Mason Museum, MI

In 1822, while living and working in Liverpool, New York, Caleb married Celinda Carey. He was twenty-two, Celinda was seventeen. Their union would produce six children, only four surviving to adulthood: Maloan (my great-great-grandmother), Mantha, Miranda and a brother Monroe. (They liked M's!)

More of a sailor than farmer, Caleb served for several years as a captain and boat owner on the Great Lakes. Like his forebears, Caleb would eventually go west. Hearing news of cheap land, good soil and good jobs due to the rise of steamboat navigation, Caleb decided to move to Michigan with Celinda and their four children in 1836. They settled in Berrien County in the newly settled township of Niles. He continued as a sea captain, as well as farming. He captained boats that ran on the St. Joseph River from 1844 to 1848. He spent three years on the steamship Star" for Mr. J. Beeson, and on the Odd Fellow for Mr. Porter Paine. The St. Joseph River (running through southern Michigan and northern Indiana) was an important transportation route for moving both passengers and commodities.

Caleb's life was a century of tangled contradictions under sixteen presidents. Michigan attracted a stream of settlers. Land was cheap, fertile and promised opportunity triggered by the 1819 Treaty of Saginaw. The federal government ceded nearly six million acres of Indian land to Michigan settlers. (In their efforts to oppose white settlement expansion, numerous Native tribes sided with the British against the U.S. government during the American Revolution and the War of 1812.) The 1819 Treaty's passage encouraged settlers to move west to St. Joseph County in southwestern Michigan and to homestead. This was in response to reports of rich prairies, but was also enhanced by the passage by Congress of "The Indian Removal Act" in 1830.

This insidious government policy, signed into law by President Andrew Jackson, provided for the legal expulsion and forced relocation of Indian tribes from their lands, allowing settlers to acquire the abandoned territory. This legislative act followed a long list of previous government laws, regulations and broken treaties. It was seeded in the legacy of early settler colonialism and was meant to force indigenous people off their lands or eradicate them.

"Michigania" was the name given to the stream of these early families who carried with them all the characteristics of their New England ancestors, including the township system, agricultural methods and certain Puritan traditions. When Caleb settled in Niles in1835, the Potawatomi Indians (members of the Algonquian family) had ceded their last bit of land to the government.

Caleb was appointed Indian agent in 1836 and served for five years. Except for those who had converted to Christianity, the reduced tribe of one hundred fifty Potawatomi were loaded into wagons in the fall of 1838 and escorted by U.S. troops to Kansas. I would like to think that as an active Mason, Caleb may have attempted to act as a "better man." But I haven't found any documentation to ensure that. So, I don't know.

His primary duties as Indian agent would have been to prevent conflicts between the settlers and the remaining tribes, to see to the proper distribution of annuities granted by the state and federal government and to oversee the licensing of the fur trade. However, many agents were known to be inefficient, cruel and dishonest, furnishing the Indians with "ardent spirits" (alcohol). The fur and pelt trade was slowly replaced by the lumber trade. Settlements grew, and with the Indian relocation west of the Mississippi nearly complete, only a few remained.

Typical 1830's log cabin. Berrien History Center, Michigan

With forests full of animals, and rivers and streams full of fish, and with rich soil, the goal of Caleb's family was to "live." Early home life would seem primitive to us, but it was comfortable for its time. The log cabin home was warmed by a central fireplace and lit by tallow candles. And when they ran out of candles, leftover rags were dipped in a saucer of grease.

Celinda spun her own yarn and made her family's clothing by hand. For her husband and son Monroe, she spun linsey cloth for shirts of cotton and wool. The shirts had a narrow binding instead of a collar, with a single button at the top, and were worn over pantaloons or jeans. The local tanner came by their farm once a year to make boots and shoes from the hides of animals. Given the hard work, their living conditions steadily improved.

Numerous nineteenth century writers embellished acts of "heroism" and "injun fighting" in pioneer myths. Andrew Jackson, "hero" of the Battle of New Orleans in 1815 and elected president in 1829;

William Henry Harrison, "hero" of the Battle of Tippecanoe in 1809; and later, George Custer of Little Big Horn were made into iconic American heroes. They were embedded in America's Manifest Destiny Doctrine and Europe's Doctrine of Discovery, where the theories of white supremacy and the validation of land grab by conquest were planted.

I assume Caleb probably embraced the views of his era. While his personal interaction and treatment of Native Americans is not known or documented, I would like to believe that he was just and fair towards his Indian neighbors. Peeling the skin back from one's history can reveal certain terrible truths. Although I didn't discover any terrible truths, the behavior and attitude of Caleb towards the Potawatomi remain unknown to me.

The first so-called common man, President Andrew Jackson, was a staunch supporter of states' rights. Old Hickory, as he was called, was tough and aggressive; he settled arguments with duels. He believed in limited federal government, but supported slavery and the dispossession, disempowerment and relocation of the Indians. Jackson's "democracy" was completed by his successor, James Polk, whose Manifest Destiny saw the completion of the extension of America from the Atlantic to the Pacific.

What were Caleb's views regarding land grants and cheap land for himself and fellow settlers, while the confiscation of the Native Peoples' land took place? Did he share his opinions with his children? Except for what was stated in his obituary, again, I don't know. His son-in-law, John Eaton Barnes, and Barnes' parents left slave-owning Virginia and Maryland to move to the Free State of Michigan. The Barnes and Ingersolls probably objected to slavery, but what did they believe about the Indians? Did they see them as less than human, accepting the view of Declaration signer Philip Livingston, who is quoted as saying to his fellow Colonial statesmen: "...that Indians should be dispossessed, and that women, servants and slaves remain dependent."

I do know that the prevalent view of the time in most of Michigan and New England was that slavery was wrong. However, the view that Native Americans were heathens, continued. This was exemplified in the omission of Native Americans in state and federal censuses. The original purpose of the census was to identify free white men owning land, who could be taxed and could vote. Blacks were recorded on the census as property, also for the purpose of taxation.

By 1860, Caleb, now sixty, maintained a farm of forty acres located at the end of Terre Coupe Road and a house on Bakertown Road in Buchanan; both were within walking distance of the town. After Celinda died in 1868, Caleb would marry twice more and eventually move with his third wife, Jane Simmons, to another forty acres he owned in Niles Township across the St. Joseph River.

Active in community affairs throughout his life, records show Caleb served as Village Trustee and Postmaster during the administration of James Buchanan. In the Berrien County Record obituary in 1892, it stated, "...Capt. Ingersoll was undoubtedly the oldest Mason in Michigan... he was present at all the meetings in those days...He had many friends and was highly respected for his honest and straight-forward character...and like a sheaf of wheat was ready for the harvest. The funeral was conducted under the auspices of the lodge he organized." Caleb's daughter, Maloan, would lay her father to rest in Three Oaks Cemetery, alongside her mother, Celinda Cary Ingersoll. At age 92, Caleb was blind at his death.

CHAPTER 7

SEVENTH GENERATION
Michigan

Maloan Ingersoll Barnes 1830 -1895

Maloan Ingersoll Barnes

CHILDREN OF MALOAN INGERSOLL
AND WILLIAM B. PERROTT: 1828-1864

Susan	(1849 -)
Eliza	(1851-1853)
Serena	(1855-)
Caleb Joyner	(1857-1858)
Hattie May	(1859-1861)
Almyr Eugene	(1861-1930)

CHILDREN OF MALOAN AND JOHN EATON BARNES

Jessie Barnes	(1869-1869)
Judd Barnes	(1870-1872)
Zella Dotte Barnes	(1874-1952)

Maloan Barnes Ingersoll

An old lady with pursed lips and ruffled white collar seemed to stare at me as I lay in bed. The sepia portrait hung in my grandmother's guest bedroom. This was in Los Angeles in the early 1950's, and was where I often had my special sleepovers. When I asked Cracker, the name I called my grandmother, "who is that scary old lady?" she smiled. "Your Civil War great-great-grandmother, Maloan Ingersoll Barnes."

Six decades later her portrait hangs in the front entry hall of my apartment. For years I wondered, where had she lived, what was her life like? My curiosity and research slowly gave me some of the answers I was seeking. My search began in Buchanan, Michigan in the Three Oaks Cemetery in 2012, where I found headstones for Maloan, her two husbands, William Perrott and John Barnes, her parents Caleb and Celinda Ingersoll, and a half dozen other relatives. I moved from stone to stone reading names, birth and death dates, and epitaphs, some barely legible, I felt a mysterious connection to Maloan, even though her large polished granite tombstone simply read:

Maloan
Wife of
J. E. Barnes
Aug. 30, 1830
Nov.17, 1895

Standing here, among the remains of my nineteenth-century ancestors, I recalled my grandmother telling me that Maloan's family went
back to "Indian Days." Her stern unsmiling look, my grandmother
said, was because they did not have dentists in Benton Harbor,
Michigan. An aging Maloan might have lost most of her teeth; in
many of the portraits and photos of that era, women and men had
the same look. Her father Caleb served as an Indian agent during the
Federal Removal and Relocation of the Potawatomi Indians between
1834 and 1842. The Potawatomi were neighbors, living in forests that
bordered the white settlements. The settlers and Indians would have
had regular interaction, as they traded animal pelts, baskets, blankets
and glass. (Did Maloan have Indian playmates? How did she feel
about seeing her neighbors herded up and sent away? Did her parents
discuss this at home? Or was it not a topic for conversation?) Given
the white cultural beliefs of the time, in step with President Jackson's
Indian Removal Act of 1830, I presume the family abided with those
beliefs. As an Indian agent, Caleb would have been obliged to obey
the provisions of the federal act.

Flushing out the details of Maloan and her family's story brought
me to the Niles, Michigan local library, where I learned how to use
a microfiche machine. I looked up John and Maloan Barnes in the
newspaper index, under "obituaries," then searched the rolls of microfiche. Threading them through the viewing machine, turning the
handle ever so slowly, the story of Maloan began to reveal itself.

Maloan Ingersoll was born in 1830, in Liverpool, a small rural town in upstate New York. This was five years after the opening of the Erie Canal and the premier run of the first locomotive on the first railroad laid in America. The canal and the steam locomotive were two engineering marvels, moving people and goods across thousands of miles of canals, forests and the Great Plains.

Called a "sprightly little hamlet" and the original home of the Onondaga Indians, Liverpool was a port village with a growing salt and boat-building industry. Caleb, Maloan's father, was a ship captain on Lake Ontario. Her mother, Celinda, kept house and farmed their small acreage. When she was six, her parents decided to immigrate to southwestern Michigan, where lands were opening up in the Northwest Territory.

In Syracuse, with four children in tow, the family boarded a "packet" boat, a seventy- by fourteen-foot passenger boat with quarters that served as lounge, dining room and sleeping areas. Maloan and her siblings probably slept outside on the deck in their bedrolls at night. The packet boats were pulled by teams of horses and mules on a towpath at a speed of five miles an hour. The fare was four cents a mile and included meals.

Erie Canal Packet Boat

Arriving in Buffalo, the family boarded a steamboat to Detroit, where, upon disembarking, they had to sleep on the floor of a warehouse, as all the public inns were full. Years later, Maloan's husband John would recount, as quoted in Lillian Avery's History of the Ingersoll Family in America, "Maloan woke during the night and said 'puppies' were biting her. The puppies were actually rats." The family continued on to Niles, Michigan, a three-day overland trip taken on a bumpy, dusty, pitted road – the new "Territorial Road," in a concord stagecoach pulled by four horses. For two hundred dollars, Caleb purchased a sixty-acre farm on the St. Joseph River.

Michigan was both a wilderness and a paradise in 1836: meadows surrounded with forests full of oak, hickory and game; the St. Joseph and Kalamazoo rivers full of salmon and steelhead fish; and soil rich for planting. Under the Federal Removal Program, the Potawatomi were forced to cede their territory, which then was sold to white settlers. The chief business of the early pioneer was to survive. Along with other settlers, the family cleared the land to build a log cabin. The house would have a dirt floor and a fireplace for warmth and light. With the bounty of the forest, along with honey, huckleberries, cranberries and bird eggs, the family lived well, salt being the only important necessity that they had to import or borrow.

These primitive conditions did not last long among the Michigan settler men and women. Log cabins were made more comfortable. Rugs were braided, quilts were made from scraps, and oil lamps lit homes. The population increased, with mills, trading posts, stores and businesses flourishing. Routines were established. A typical mid-day heavy dinner consisted of salt pork fried to a crisp, potatoes with milk gravy, a Johnny Cake (a cornmeal flatbread served with country butter) and pie. Coffee, sugar and tea were luxuries but soon became necessities as the communities grew.

Clothes were practical. The emphasis was not on any kind of fashion, but on warmth and durability. Men wore loose cloth shirts, called wamus, and pantaloons made of jean, a combination of linen and wool. Women made dresses from homespun linsey. The spinning wheel, ranging from four to six feet in diameter, was the largest piece of furniture in the home. Maloan, as the oldest of four children, would have been instructed in the use of the wheel as a young child, possibly taking over the spinning responsibilities. The shoemaker came around once a year to make boots and shoes. Men's boots were made from the hides of elk and white-tailed deer, which when wet and dried were as stiff as a board.

As a toughened settler's daughter at age twenty, it would have been customary for Maloan to spin, sew, cook, plow the fields and shoot a rifle. Education was done at home. In 1850, it seems she met and married William B. Perrott, an Irishman from New York. How and where? It's reasonable to assume they met in church, which was where most young women had the opportunity to meet prospective husbands. Often the unions were arranged by the parents. Settling on a small farm in Buchanan near her parents, the couple had five children, two surviving to adulthood.

Throughout the 1850's and 1860's, most families in the St. Joseph Valley lived on small independent farms, believing themselves to be the happiest and luckiest people in the world, according to several historians of the era. The town systems emulated those of their ancestors from New York and Massachusetts. Life was centered on church, home, school and the Meeting House, where disputes concerning cattle running, land disputes, water rights, Indian trading disputes and the selling of gun powder, were resolved. It was an agricultural frontier. Men and women worked side by side in the field. But what seemed a bucolic landscape was to be torn apart as war was brewing. It was a war over slavery, pitting the industrial north against the agricultural, slave-owning South. This war would interrupt Maloan's life and forever change America.

When the Civil War broke out, the conscripted men of Buchanan were organized in nearby Niles, Michigan and mustered into Union service in March 1862. A conscription system existed that allowed for a substitute, with payment of three hundred dollars, typically beyond the means of most farmers and workers. Maloan was thirty-two when she and her husband, brother and brother-in-law, went off to war, leaving her children, Suzanna, Fletcher and Almyr, with her sixty-two-year-old father, Caleb.

William B. Perrott & Maloan Ingersoll Perrott
Buchanan, Michigan 1860

Getting to the battlefields was no easy matter. Each town was required to fund its quota of troops, as well as provide uniforms, rifles and food. When Maloan and William left Buchanan in 1862, they traveled by train to St. Louis, then by steamer on the Mississippi, Ohio and Tennessee rivers, finally reaching Pittsfield, and ultimately landing in southwestern Tennessee where the western war was being conducted under the Union command of Ulysses S. Grant. They arrived in time to take part in the Battle of Shiloh, on the 6th and 7th of April, at the site of the Shiloh Church in a field of blossoming peaches. The first day of battle saw the Confederate army deliver a crushing blow to the Union troops, only to retreat the next day. A two-day bloodbath ensued, where a staggering 13,000 Federalist troops were lost and 10,000 Confederates. One of the bloodiest battles of the Civil War, the brigades, divisions and corps were green, with no actual field experience, few having even fired a musket rife. Pushed to the front and overwhelmed by the rush of the enemy, they naively shouted out a popular chant at that time:

"We're fighting for the Union
We're fighting for the trust
We're fighting for the happy land
Where sleeps our fathers dust"

Maloan and other wives accompanied their husbands to the front, a custom that began during the American Revolution. William Perrott was a first lieutenant, and officers got somewhat better accommodations than the enlisted men. Maloan would have stayed in a single officer's tent with her husband, which provided privacy and a bit of comfort. Short furloughs often allowed the couple to spend time in nearby comfortable taverns with better food. The women provided companionship, washing, nursing and cooking. Between battles and to fight off the monotony of daily battle drills and labor details, Maloan and other officers' wives would arrange dances, band concerts and amateur shows. The soldiers would organize chess and checker games, ball games, and foot and horseraces in which officers participated.

But life for all the troops was miserable. There were frequent storms, mud, dysentery and lack of adequate supplies. Food rations or "grub" consisted of rice and beans and, more often, "hardtack," hard rock flour crackers and stale coffee. Enlisted men slept on bedrolls in open fields with their muskets and the whine of mosquitoes as bedfellows. Rations of liquor were given to anyone volunteering for burial duty.

The battered Union troops from Shiloh would soon claim victory at Vicksburg, the last Confederate stronghold, in a siege that lasted forty-seven days. Capture of Vicksburg, a port city of five thousand people, allowed the Union to take control of the Mississippi, blockading the southern seaports. This was the North's key to winning the war. The Michigan twelfth regiment took its battle position high on Hayne's Bluff overlooking the Mississippi River. The command of this campaign fell to Ulysses S. Grant and William T. Sherman, the latter being associated with Sherman's famous March to the Sea, where he destroyed everything in his path from Atlanta to Savannah.

It was on the decks of a steam transport ship anchored at the bottom of the Vicksburg fortress that I envision Maloan. She would have heard the deafening battle sounds and seen the blinding fireworks of gunboats, ironclads and canons bombarding the Mississippi city. She would have witnessed Vicksburg men, women and children suffer under the constant shelling from Grant's heavy guns. The starving civilians were forced to move out of their homes into surrounding hills where they lived in caves. All this in the hot and humid Mississippi summer where the average daily temperature was ninety-eight and tiny chiggers would burrow under a person's skin. The residents of Vicksburg waited in vain for a military rescue.

Grant and Sherman took ravaged Vicksburg on July 6, 1863, two days after the more famous battle of Gettysburg on July 4, 1863. General Lee would lose one third of his army at Gettysburg, with 29,500 Confederate soldiers surrendering, the largest surrender of American troops in the nation's history.

I imagine Maloan standing by her husband in a large viewing crowd on that July 4 morning, watching the surrender ceremony. General Grant and the Confederate General, John Pemberton, were dressed in civilian clothes as they signed the surrender agreement. The ceremony would not make it to the front page of the Harpers Weekly newspaper for another month, accompanied by an artist's sketch of the occasion. Maloan must have felt relief and had thoughts of going home. She was away from her three children and family for two of the war's five years. Of the 2,325 men who left Buchanan as part of the Twelfth Union regiment, 432 were killed in action, dying from wounds or disease.

Detailing the deplorable hospital conditions in Washington D.C., the writer Louisa May Alcott wrote about her experience caring for wounded soldiers in Sketches. She described the conditions for the soldiers as worse than the battlefield, disease taking twice as many lives as bullet wounds. This was understandable, considering the swampy water and muddy terrain of the Mississippi and Tennessee rivers. They were breeding grounds for mosquitoes, ticks, chiggers, ague and malaria. These were the conditions in Vicksburg where Maloan assisted doctors in surgery. Given the many historical descriptions of medical field operations, I picture Maloan, witnessing surgeons with unwashed hands amputating soldiers' limbs with filthy instruments, unclean sponges and lint to soak up the blood, dirty handkerchiefs and stained uniforms to bind wounds when no clean cloth was available. (Amidst the violence, I've tried to imagine the inner life of Maloan. Was she war hardened? Did she witness any of the cruelty by plantation owners? What did she think about the war and slavery?)

After being furloughed in February 1864, Maloan and her husband William made the long arduous trip home to Buchanan by water, train and wagon. Suffering from battle wounds, as well as from consumption (tuberculosis), William died shortly after he arrived home. In all, over 600,000 Union and Confederate soldiers died in this the bloodiest of America's wars.

*"Men whose glossy hair
Grew grey on the edge of the grave,
Who lie so humbly there,
Because you were so grand and brave."* *

Maloan remained on the couple's farm in Buchanan with her children and family after William died. A list of household and farm items in William's estate included:

"One horse eight years	*115.00*
one light wagon	*40.00*
one single harness	*25.00*
one cow eight years old	*20.00*
one sofa	*30.00*
two tables	*9.00 ..."*

The following year, in 1865, Maloan's eighteen-year-old daughter, Suzanna Perrott died. Suzanna's husband, John Barnes, was returning to Buchanan after being mustered out of military service. Maloan nurtured the heartbroken John back to life, and two years later, in 1867, she married her son-in-law. She was thirty-seven, and he was twenty-five. I have made the assumption that this probably was a marriage of convenience and necessity. Maloan secured a provider for her children and overseer of two farms, while John acquired a homemaker and an able partner.

After losing two children in infancy, the couple buried John's parents, John and Anna Barnes, in 1870 and 1871. They then left Buchanan and went to Howard City, Kansas for two years. John had acquired land as a result of the Homestead Act of 1860 and wanted to start a new life in a new place. This is where Maloan, at age forty-four, gave birth to a daughter, Zella Dotte Barnes, my great-grandmother. (Was Maloan embarrassed about her marriage to her son-in- law and being his senior by twelve years? Was she eager to get away from local town gossip, encouraging the move to Howard City?) Whatever the reason, the couple returned to Buchanan in 1874.

Buchanan and the surrounding towns in Berrien Country experienced a shifting economy during the late nineteenth and early twentieth century. Farm-related industries gave way to industrial production and an expanding fruit industry. Buchanan saw the growth of mills, streetcars, telegraph service, canals, and boat and ferry service. Maloan spent the next three decades helping John build the Spencer Barnes Furniture Manufacturing Company, first in Buchanan, then later in Benton Harbor where the couple moved in 1891 with their only surviving child, Dotte. With a population of seventeen hundred, Benton Harbor had it all: Bell Block pharmaceuticals, the Palladium Newspaper, the First National Bank, the American House Hotel, Morrison & Cullinine's Dry Goods Store, the Bell Opera House, the Le Chic lounge and the Lunt Central Music House, which sold a full line of embroidery supplies, musical merchandise, pianos, sheet music, records and talking machines.

Maloan and John were considered eminent and prosperous citizens of both Buchanan and Benton Harbor. They built their Queen Anne, wood-shingle house on Morton Hill above Territorial Avenue. It was across the street from Eleazar Morton's home, one of the city's founders. Surrounded by acres of peach, apple and pear orchards, Maloan raised my great-grandmother Dotte, and even had Dotte's portrait painted. The St. Joseph Valley became known as the best fruit region of the Northwest. In 1897, the Morrill Peach Orchard was named the "finest peach orchard in America" by the American Horticultural Society. An annual spring peach festival continues today over one hundred years later, celebrating the peach orchards. (No wonder I am a fastidious gardener!)

Surviving the ravages of civil war, the death of a husband and five of her children, bearing witness to the end of the retreating wilderness and the advancing American frontier of 1892 (as all government land was spoken for), Maloan, at seventy-five, died of complications from typhoid fever in November of 1895. In that same year, her grandchild, my grandmother Nurma Nadjy, was one year old.

The November 19, 1895 obituary for Maloan in Benton Harbor's local newspaper, The Palladium, reported, "… the deceased was frequently at the front with her husband, Capt. Wm. B. Perrott and participated in some of the most thrilling events of that period, having been on board one of the Union ships when she was fired upon by the Confederacy. She witnessed the hanging of a rebel spy, and was associated with some of the bravest spirits of those trying days. … Many a sick soldier received kind attention at her hands. …"

Maloan's life was marked by three large historical events: The end of the Civil War and slavery; the confiscation and resettlement of Native peoples; and the beginning of rights for women in the Victorian era. I'd like to think that Maloan was well-informed and emboldened in her outlook and behavior by the progress made by the brave ladies of the Seneca Falls, New York Convention for Women's Rights in 1848. That convention was capped off in 1872 with the nomination of the first female for president of the United States, Virginia Woodhull. I don't know about Maloan's thinking – did she agree with the prevailing white and national attitudes toward women, freed Black people and the Native people?

In closing this chapter on this remarkable woman's life, book-ended in flowering peach fields, I realize my generation of the 1960's did not begin the Women's Movement. It was Maloan's generation that helped pave the way. When I pass by Maloan's portrait now, I feel I know her a bit better, and I smile with pride.

CHAPTER 8

SIXTH GENERATION
Virginia, Maryland & Michigan

John Eli Barnes 1790-1872
Anna Ross Barnes 1808-1871

Armory at Harpers Ferry, Virginia, 1800

CHILDREN OF JOHN ELI BARNES & FIRST WIFE (UNKNOWN)

Samuel Barnes
Jacob Barnes

CHILDREN OF JOHN ELI BARNES AND HANNAH YASTE

Elizabeth Barnes	(1820-1895)
Mahala Adelia Barnes	(1818-1892)
Rebecca Ellen Barnes	(1828-1906)

CHILDREN OF JOHN AND ANNA (WEST) BARNES

John Eaton Barnes	(1842-1917)
Franklin Barnes	(1852-)

CHILDREN OF ANNA (ROSS) WEST AND ABRAHAM WEST

Fletcher West	(1832-1916)
Isaac Pembroke West	(1833-1915

John Eli Barnes (date unknown)

John Eli Barnes

John Eli Barnes' Virginia parentage remains a mystery. Attempting to solve it, I visited Shepherdstown, West Virginia in October 2014. Originally Mecklenburg, it was renamed Shepherdstown in 1820 in honor of its founder John Shepherd. In my eyes, the town is an American treasure – looking much the same as it did two hundred years ago, thanks to funding for restoration efforts. Shepherdstown is the oldest town in West Virginia and a stone's throw (twelve miles) from Harpers Ferry, West Virginia. John Barnes was raised there.

This is the Harpers Ferry where, in 1859, Abolitionist John Brown led his famous raid in an attempt to gather arms for the enslaved Black people.

Harpers Ferry sits on a V-shaped water gap where the Potomac cuts through the Blue Ridge at the meeting point of the Potomac and Shenandoah rivers. The location made it a natural corridor for commercial mills and an armory complex, the second largest armory after Springfield, Massachusetts. John Eli Barnes would have been a boy of thirteen in 1803 when Merriweather Lewis came to Harpers Ferry to buy arms and supplies for the famous Lewis and Clark expedition. Later, John worked on one of the flat boats drawn by horses and mules that moved people, animals and goods on the Potomac and Shenandoah rivers.

Walking the historic town and visiting the local historical society in the old Endicott Hotel, I spent an afternoon with the museum curator. There was a large Barnes family contingent in the Shepherdstown area. All indications are that my John was part of the John and Joseph Barnes family who arrived from England and settled in the Shenandoah Valley prior to the American Revolution. But the documents remain inconclusive, and I've made several assumptions.

John Barnes married young. Nothing is known of his first wife. In a copy of his will there is mention of two children: Jacob Barnes of Missouri and Samuel R. Barnes of Baltimore. The will also mentions children with a second wife, Hannah Yeast. Records show John Barnes marrying Hannah Yeast (Yates/Yost) in Frederick County in (1813 and 1817) and having three daughters, Elizabeth, Mahala and Rebecca. Then with yet a third wife, Anna (West) Ross, he had two sons: John Eaton Barnes and Franklin Barnes, both belonging to my maternal ancestral line, who would eventually marry into my Michigan Ingersoll family.

One thing you can usually find is a census. One from 1820 has John living in Frederick County, Maryland, across the river from Harpers Ferry. In 1830, another census lists him living in Middletown, Frederick County, working with Isaac Eaton in his blacksmith shop. The Barnes and Eaton families were neighbors, co-workers and they possibly worshiped together. A local Frederick County newspaper abstract under John's name reads: "runaway negro apprentice Patrick Hart age 18 blacksmith businesses in Middletown." I assume John posted this in hopes of getting Patrick back. Blacks had economic value; they were treated as property and taxed.

Several book citations also show the Eatons immigrating to South Bend in St. Joseph County, Indiana in 1831. Four years later, John immigrated to South Bend. I assume John received letters from his friend Isaac, extolling the positive attributes of St. Joseph County. But the move was probably also for anti-slavery reasons and, along with improved transportation, the promise of less expensive and more fertile land. Government land was selling for a dollar and a quarter an acre in the Northwest Territory, encouraging immigration, the government and military having forcibly relocated indigenous tribes to west of the Mississippi and Kansas.

From my maternal grandmother I inherited an original, hand-written commission, dated 1826, from President Polk at Annapolis when John was made captain in the 28ᵗʰ Regiment of the Maryland Militia of Frederick County. Additional records show that John served as Justice of the Peace in Frederick County, Maryland. Still, the question must be asked: Was he sympathetic to slavery?

I found a copy of a bill of "land sale of a Negro girl dated October 22, 1821" in an internet data base but no additional purchase agreements. It was common for households to have a Black household "servant." Although the bill shows that the "servant" was owned and thus enslaved. On the other hand, John did relocate. This encourages me to believe John was against slavery, or at least not supporting its expansion. Up until Michigan's acceptance as a state in 1837, it was part of the larger land area known as the Northwest Territory. Although slavery was forbidden in the Territory, the expulsion of the indigenous people by the government was endorsed.

How did John and his family get to South Bend? Perhaps he would have traveled on the newly completed C&O Canal, and then on the National Cumberland Road, which was dotted with numerous inns where the travelers could rest and get a meal for twenty-five cents. Or perhaps they made the journey by steamboat up the Mississippi to the Ohio and Illinois rivers, and then to the Kankakee River that ended near South Bend. Traveling north or south on those rivers made South Bend, perched high on the banks of the St. Joseph River, an attractive destination. Or maybe, just maybe, they traveled by wagons, north to St. Louis, north to Ft. Wayne and South Bend on the Fort Wayne Highway, part of the Old Chicago Road. It was hard going in either case.

The newly arriving Barnes family might have been welcomed with the Eatons in South Bend, and then with the Isaac Ross family, where John would meet and marry his third wife, Anna West Ross. In Timothy Edward Howard's book, History of St. Joseph County, it states that the second Mrs. Barnes died sometime after moving to South Bend. "Hannah Yeast of German descent ... died before her family's home was established in this county...and...Father (of Elizabeth Barnes) having made the journey with his 2nd wife."

Land records show that Center Township, Indiana is where John, Anna and their blended family initially settled on forty acres in St. Joseph County (which included parts of northern Indiana and southern Michigan). Although the prairies were rich for planting and harvesting and there were always game and fowl, there were many discomforts on the frontier, especially death and disease. And, there were the Native peoples who remained.

My family would have had knowledge of the Indian Wars. The Black Hawk War in 1832 opposed President Jackson's legislation of 1830 to remove the majority of the tribes west of the Mississippi. The Barnes family arrived in South Bend two years after the tragic "Trail of Death" march, the forced removal of the Miami and Potawatomi Indian tribes from northern Indiana and Michigan to the Osage River in Kansas. By 1840, the town had few Indians. The number of settlers in St. Joseph neared seven thousand.

Anna (West) Ross was the fifth child of fourteen children of Isaac and Elizabeth Pembroke West. When she met John she was a widow with two children. Anna may have joined the Barnes caravan west to Indiana, intending to join her Ross family. Within five years she became John's third wife. It was common for settlers in America to be married several times and have many children. Women died frequently in childbirth as there was no contraception. And children were needed to work the family farms.

John had both blacksmith and carpentry skills. Records indicate that John worked in Isaac Eaton's and Clem Studebaker's South Bend blacksmith shop, living in various St. Joseph townships for twenty-five years. In South Bend the Barnes-Eaton ties grew stronger. Two of John's daughters, Elizabeth and Mahala, married Isaac Eaton's two sons, brothers Jacob and John Eaton. In 1860, at seventy, John and fifty-two-year-old Anna would move to Buchanan, Michigan where their son John Jr. was living. They would remain there the rest of their lives.

John Eli Barnes

Born in 1790 during George Washington's second year of office, John Barnes would live through twelve presidencies, including the completion of Thomas Jefferson's and James Polk's vision of a land acquisition, the assassination of Abraham Lincoln, and the soon to be completed expulsion and relocation of America's indigenous people. And their son John Eaton Barnes would marry into my Michigan Ingersoll family.

CHAPTER 9

EIGHTH GENERATION
Michigan

John Eaton Barnes 1842-1917

John Eaton Barnes, circa 1914

CHILDREN OF JOHN EATON BARNES

Jessie Barnes	(1869-1869)
Judd Barnes	(1870-1872)
Zella Dotte Barnes	(1874-1952)

"Death of John Barnes Ends An Active Life"...
Berrien County lost one of her best known and most
admired business men ... Benton Harbor man was a pioneer, soldier, manufacturer, banker, public servant ..."

Niles Daily Sun, November 3, 1917, Benton Harbor, Michigan

John Eaton Barnes

On a cool Saturday afternoon in September 2014, my sister Lisa
Marcato and I drove up and down deserted streets of downtown Benton Harbor, Michigan. We were looking for remnants
of the Spencer & Barnes furniture factory where John Barnes, our
great-great-grandfather's manufacturing plant was located at the inter-
section of Paw Paw Avenue and Main Street.

Checkered with abandoned, weed-covered lots, Main Street was
lined with bleak gray buildings. We did find a small art district in
the middle of downtown that we were told was leading the way to an
economic resurgence. We gazed at the once famous St. Vincent Hotel
where Al Capone summered, now, ironically, a sad-looking government building. Then, on the side of a forlorn building, straining our
eyes in the mid-day sun, we made out the faded script: Spencer &
Barnes Furniture Company.

During the late nineteenth and early twentieth centuries, when
our Barnes family lived here, it was a thriving industrial town. Clark

Equipment, Upjohn Machine Company (now Whirlpool) and the Spencer & Barnes furniture factory lined busy streets. Originally built on a ship canal, dug from the St. Joseph River, the town of Benton Harbor was where Great Lake ships delivered goods. The city was incorporated in 1891. That year, John Barnes moved his family to a newly built home directly across the street from the Morton home on Territorial Avenue. The Mortons were early settlers and one of Benton Harbor's most prominent families, with which John partnered in city development projects.

Now, in 2014, Benton Harbor was not noteworthy, a shadow of its former self. We decided to explore Buchanan, a twenty-minute drive south, where John Barnes had lived and worked for over four decades. We spent the afternoon threading microfiche through tiny black metal spools in the Buchanan Public Library and looking at old photos, separated by thin tissue paper in large flat cardboard boxes. We did this with the help of Robert Brown, president of Three Oaks Cemetery where our Barnes family members are interred. Over lunch in the Union Café luncheonette on Front Street, Robert told us about the area, originally the Northwest Territory. He encouraged us to visit the nearby History Center and phoned to arrange an introduction with the curator, Robert Meyer.

A short distance east of Buchanan, we found the Berrien Springs History Center. The compound consists of the oldest court house in Michigan, dating back to 1839, as well as several smaller historic structures, including an early nineteenth century restored log cabin. At the History Center, we climbed a steep flight of rickety stairs where we were greeted by Robert Meyer. He handed us a treasure trove of documents in five, dust-covered file boxes. Goosebumps rose on our arms, an occasional gasp interrupting our silence as we perused the documents, discovering fresh and tantalizing information about our family. This is what genealogy is all about!

It turned out that John Barnes had a third wife we hadn't known about. His father John Sr., in turn, had two children from an unknown first marriage in Virginia – this we did not know. For several hours, we reverently handled and read wills, deeds, letters, invoices and legal notices.

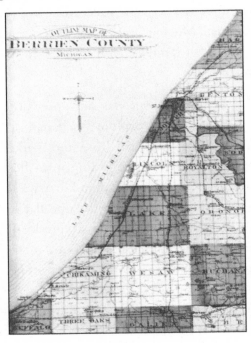

Berrien County-St. Joseph Valley, Michigan

The triangle that encompasses Benton Harbor, Buchanan and Berrien Springs is nestled among rolling hills, open fields and verdant green farms. Nearby are Lake Michigan and the St. Joseph River. The landscape reminded us of New England. Our Massachusetts Ingersoll ancestors must have appreciated the similarities. We found Buchanan to be a handsome town, well preserved with its nineteenth century village buildings and the Pears Mill, a restored mid-nineteenth century flour mill. Retail shops on Front Street were open and filled with shoppers and tourists visiting the mill. Buchanan clearly had done a successful job in revitalizing its downtown. With Robert Brown's knowledge of the area's history and curator Meyer's help, we began to piece together the life of Benton Harbor and Buchanan, when John Eaton Barnes lived there.

Born in 1842, John and his parents, John and Anna, made their home in the wilderness near South Bend, Indiana. John Jr. acquired his early education by walking two and half miles to a log schoolhouse on Palmers Prairies, and was taught by Clem Studebaker of the South Bend Studebaker Wagon Works, later the Studebaker Automobile Company. In 1850, Clem Studebaker opened a blacksmith shop making farm wagons; he hired John when John turned eight. Here, John would acquire the foundation skills for a future furniture man-ufacturer. In 1854, when John was twelve, his parents left Indiana and settled in Niles township, four miles south of Berrien Springs, Michigan. He would remain with his family on their seventeen-acre farm until the family moved to Buchanan in 1858, where John lived until the outbreak of the Civil War.

John left his aging parents in August of 1864, the final year of the Civil War. At age twenty-two, conscripted along with Barnes, Ingersoll and the Perrott families and neighbors, he joined the 12th Michigan Union Infantry, Company I. The "Rowdy Michigonians" would earn the reputation of being among the most ferocious fight-ers of the war because of their rugged frontier background and their excellent marksmanship. By the time John joined the army, most of the major Civil War campaigns were over. John and his fellow soldiers marched long distances, fighting small skirmishes, performing endless drills and standing daily guard duty.

John kept a small pocket diary, dated 1864, which he wrote in almost daily. I know this because it was given to me by my grandmother, Cracker. In it, he describes daily drills, hunting for rabbits, the weather, letters he wrote home and received weekly from his mother Anna Barnes, his friend Monroe Ingersoll and wife "Susie" Perrott. There is no mention of slaves, slavery or Black soldiers. This small faded treasure connects me to John Barnes every time I touch it.

Michigan was a Free State, having fought on the side of the Union. In 1848, in Jackson, Michigan, the Republican Party was founded. The party was often referred to as the Party of Lincoln. Whatever John's thinking was about slavery, it is not revealed in his diary entries. His father, John Sr., had left the slave state of Virginia for Michigan. Were the family anti-slavery proponents? I don't know.

Diary Entry – Civil War – February 1864

When John's military term expired in August 1865, he returned home to care for his aging parents and, according to Lillian Avery's Ingersoll genealogy, "thus repaying them by filial love and devotion for the care which they had bestowed upon him in his youth." In Buchanan, John began his business of home furnishings for the returning veterans and their families.

His wife Susie died soon after John returned home, after which he poured himself into work. First as a carpenter and then, in 1868, for the Black Manufacturing Company. The Black furniture factory was where John refined his woodworking skills that would later be patented. During this period John was comforted over the loss of his wife by her mother, Maloan Perrott. They would marry in 1867. He was twenty-five and Maloan thirty-seven. The couple settled on the Barnes family farm in Buchanan along with John's mother and father, three children and a housekeeper. Maloan oversaw two family farms, her late husband's and the Barnes farm. John continued working at the Black furniture factory until 1871.

After burying his parents, John Sr. in 1870 and Anna in 1871, John and Maloan moved to Howard City, Kansas. John had sixty acres of land from land grants the government offered men in exchange for their military service. He farmed there for two years, returning to Buchanan to work again for the Black Manufacturing Company, and later at Willard & Spencer.

At Willard & Spencer John advanced his knowledge of furniture manufacturing with his partner Benajah Spencer. In a building twenty-four by forty feet, the two men turned a lathe, a ripsaw and planer with a four- horse engine and boiler, making extension hat racks. The business grew and John bought half interest in Willard in 1875, becoming "Spencer & Barnes." The factory would manufacture bedroom sets, chiffoniers, dressers and desks, eventually employing a hundred Buchanan workers.

John built "Spencer & Barnes," becoming president when he moved the plant to Benton Harbor in 1891. He moved the plant into a structure on Paw Paw Avenue, with a wing of about six hundred feet on North Street. Built in 1890, the building had been one of the oldest in the city. The company became the town's largest employer, with two hundred skilled mechanics, using one million feet of hardwood a month to make bedroom furniture, tables, candlesticks and floor lamps.

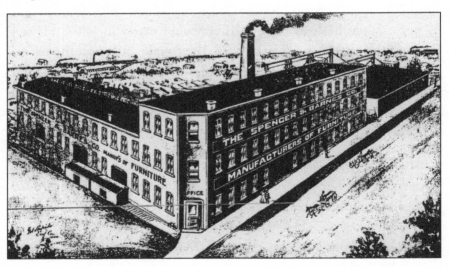

Spencer Barnes Manufacturing Company – Benton Harbor 1892

When the factory burned to the ground on July 22, 1935, "… it created a blaze that lit the heavens drawing a crowd of 3, 000," according to the newspaper of the day.

Even though Benton Harbor eclipsed the Niles and Buchanan areas as a manufacturing center, John wanted to retain a presence in

Buchanan, so in 1892 with two partners, W.S. Wells and Alfred Richards, John organized another stock furniture company, the Buchanan Cabinet Company. By 1905 it was the largest factory in Buchanan. Located on the corner of Days Avenue and First Street, it manufactured sideboards, desks, bookcases, kitchen and sewing cabinets. It closed in 1918. In addition to his factories, John was President of the Benton Harbor Development Company, a principal in the building of the Benton Harbor Ship Canal, the "first street railway," which in 1885 was pulled by mules between St. Joseph and Benton Harbor, replaced by the railroad in 1906. In 1907, John became the President of the American National Bank. He served as an education board member in Benton Harbor and Buchanan, as an alderman, a member of the board of public works and a long-standing member of the Oddfellows. For thirty of his forty years in furniture manufacturing, Maloan was his partner, reconciling accounts, overseeing the payroll and caring for the family and farms.

Board of Supervisors – Berrien County, Michigan, 1907

In 1895, Maloan contracted typhoid fever, a devastating, common disease, as did her daughter, Dotte. Dotte lived but Maloan died. John was left alone in his territorial home with Dotte and her young child, Nurma Nadjy, my grandmother. Two years after Maloan's death, John married Lucretia Partridge Adams whom he met at a furniture show in Chicago. Lucretia had two daughters, Grace, age ten, and Gertrude, thirteen. They moved into the Queen Anne family home on Morton Hill surrounded by apple, peach, plum and apricot orchards. The new Mrs. Barnes assumed the role as head of household. This included Dotte and Nurma Nadjy. Dotte's husband Charles Ortland, a Swedish "confectioner," had abandoned them.

The new Mrs. Barnes brought disharmony. To maintain peace, John built another Queen Anne-style house and moved with his wife Lucretia, two step-daughters and mother-in-law, three blocks away to Edwards Avenue in 1910. When he died in 1917, he left a large estate in a prospering town.

This elusive, ambitious and, I think, rather rigid great-great-grand-father of mine lived through great changes in the second half of the nineteenth century – the abolition of slavery, the Indian wars in the Plains and unparalleled inventions. He drove around Benton Harbor in his Henry Ford Model T. The automobile ended the supremacy of the train, giving Americans the freedom to go wherever they wished. The telephone allowed the young women in the family to speak with boyfriends in privacy. The incandescing light bulb replaced the dirty, burning oil lanterns, and gaslights safely illuminated homes for reading, board games and card playing. In the 1950's in Los Angeles, my grandmother Cracker would teach me how to play poker and gin rummy by electric light.

Returning to the Three Oaks Cemetery at the end of our visit, standing beside the large granite stone that interred John and Maloan,

I felt I knew them. Their epitaphs were simple with full column tributes in the Niles Daily Sun and Buchanan Palladium, recording the lives of these two remarkable people, my Civil War great-great-grandparents. Born in the wilderness, both John and Maloan saw the end of the frontier, went to war, made furniture for the middle class, used inventions that changed America, all the while presiding over several blended families. It is hard for me to envisage their internal lives, feelings and thoughts. It was an era when matters concerning sex, slavery and Indians were rarely discussed by settlers. The male-dominated county courtroom was where issues and positions were deliberated and infractions adjudicated. White supremacy norms were embedded in cultural standards, rooted in law.

Barnes Family Monument
Three Oaks Cemetery, Berrien County, Michigan

CHAPER 10

NINTH GENERATION
Michigan & California

Zella Dotte Barnes 1874-1952

Zella Dotte Barnes (circa 1898) Benton Harbor, Michigan

CHILD OF ZELLA DOTTE BARNES & CHARLES ORTLAND

Nurma Nadjy (Ortland/Waite) (1894-1972)

SECOND HUSBAND WILLIAM S. WAITE (1867-1968)

Zella Dotte Barnes

My great-grandmother, Mimi, was recognizable everywhere by her mountaintop of snow-white hair. In 1953, I visited Mimi in her apartment on Wilshire Boulevard in Los Angeles. She was ill and dying at age seventy-eight. I sat on her bed as she stroked my hand and smiled at me through her large, blue-gray eyes. But it was the snow-white hair that fascinated me. My grandmother told me, "my mother's hair turned silver-white by the time she was twenty-eight."

Mimi had lived in Benton Harbor, Michigan where she raised her daughter "Cracker." Mimi's husband, Charles Ortland, a handsome Swedish "confectioner" left shortly after Nurma was born. Mimi (Dotte) and Nurma remained with Dotte's parents, Maloan and John Barnes, in the old house on Territorial Road. The two-story wood-shingled home on Morton Hill survives, albeit shabby and diminished from its former grandeur.

The 1890's ended in a long depression. Most families struggled, including the Barnes family. Six thousand U.S. firms went bankrupt, one fifth of the work force was unemployed, and debt-laden farmers were being foreclosed. Racial conflicts remained and the violence between U.S. soldiers and the Indians continued unabated until the end of the century. The massacres at the Battle of Little Big Horn with George Custer in 1876, followed by the tragic slaughter of the Lakota in South Dakota at Wounded Knee in 1887, remain indelible in American history. Compounding the violence and forced Indian removal was the Dawes Act of 1887, which authorized the president to survey Indian lands and divide them into allotments for individual Indians. This U.S. legislation completed the dismantling of many of the Native tribes and land. I wondered if my ancestors saw slavery and Indian policy as abhorrent, and wanted to be in a more compassionate territory, so left Kansas in order to return to the free state of Michigan, or had they just wanted to return to their families and fertile farmland? I do not know, but I'd like to think both.

Whatever their reason, John and Maloan returned to Buchanan in 1875 to pursue cabinet and furniture making. They traveled back to Buchanan with one-year-old Dotte on a combination of rivers and the iron horse. Prior to the Civil War it took three months in covered wagons to cross the U.S, now the journey took six days via the railroad that was completed in 1869.

The middle class grew rapidly after the Civil War, including the Barnes family, who lived first in Buchanan and then in Benton Harbor. Mimi went to the schoolhouse dubbed Fort Sumter in Buchanan, as it looked like a military fortress. A three-story stone building, it had a slate roof and a belfry that housed a four-hundred-pound bell. The school had eight classrooms, a lecture hall and accommodated over five hundred students at the end of Dotte's first year of high school.

Fort Sumter, Buchanan, MI

Buchanan Class of 1890

In 1891, Dotte was uprooted again from her friends and neighbors, when her father moved the family and the Spencer & Barnes furniture plant to Benton Harbor. Within two years of the move, at age nineteen, Dotte was married and pregnant with my grandmother.

Dotte remained in the Barnes family home and in 1898 married her second husband, William S. Waite. Dotte was twenty-four and William Waite (Gramps) was thirty-one. Waite owned and operated Waite's Furniture Store on Main Street in downtown Benton Harbor, selling furniture, rugs, men's clothes and stoves. Within two years of Maloan's death, Mimi's father, John Barnes, took a third wife, Lucretia Adams, and adopted her two daughters. This new family arrangement must have been challenging for the young couple as census records of 1900 show Dotte and William living in a boarding house in Chicago. They soon returned to the territorial home to raise 6-year-old-Nurma.

With the beginning of the new century, and during the hot summers, I imagine Dotte and William taking Nurma on boat excursions up the St. Joseph River to Buchanan's Rough Opera House. The "Rough" was an entertainment hall. Located at the corner of Front and Oak streets in downtown Buchanan, its third floor heard Elizabeth Cady Stanton lift her voice in defense of women, and South Bend, Indiana newspaperman Schuyler Colfax, vice president under Grant, give a lecture on President Lincoln. It is where Nurma saw her first motion pictures, inspiring her years later, to leave Michigan for Hollywood. Both the Barnes and Waite families were prosperous. By 1908, the families were taking trips in their new sedan convertible automobile to Ingersoll, Canada, to visit relatives, riding the train to Chicago for the landscapes of Thomas Eaton and Winslow Homer, where the oil portrait of Maloan, taken from an old photograph, was commissioned.

The blended household must have been challenging. In 1911, when Nurma went off to St. Mary's College in South Bend, Indiana, Dotte and Gramps moved out of the territorial home and into the Dwan Hotel and Bath House, the four-story brick building at the corner of Territorial and Fifth. At the time of the hotel's completion in 1912, at a cost of $100,000, it was the largest in southwestern Michigan. It boasted one hundred guest rooms, an elevator stopping at each floor, a telephone in every room, and thirty-two tubs in the bathhouse. According to a family friend, Mary Jane Dillon, it was while living at the Dwan in the late 1920s and 1930s that Dotte went downstairs "every night to smoke and play poker with the men. Can you imagine your great-grandmother, the only woman in that smoke-filled, mahogany-paneled room with those gangsters?" The "Buster from Chicago" Al Capone spent the hot summer months down the street at the St. Vincent Hotel, regularly joining the card games at the Dwan Hotel. Mary Jane claimed Dotte attended Capone's going-away party at the St. Vincent before he went off to Leavenworth Penitentiary in 1931.

After Nurma graduated from St. Mary's, she married wealthy merchant Ralph Huesman in Los Angeles in 1916. Mimi and William Waite escaped much of Michigan's cold winters when they accompanied their daughter and her husband on their annual transatlantic trips to Europe. Records show the Waites and Huesmans sailing regularly from New York to France and England throughout the 1920's and 1930's on the Aquitania, Berengaria and Mauritania. I have 16-millimeter films showing them boarding ships and riding camels in formal clothes with the pyramids in the background. Dotte would eventually be persuaded to move to sun-drenched Los Angeles in 1935, after selling Waite's store to William and Jack Hearn, the brothers of family friend Mary Jane Dillon.

R. M. S. "AQUITANIA"

CAPTAIN
E. G. DIGGLE, R.D., R.N.R.

STAFF CAPTAIN
R. A. ALEXANDER, D.S.O., R.D., R.N.R.

OFFICERS

Chief Engineer......L. Roberts	*Chief Officer*......W. C. Ba...
Staff Ch. Engineer..H. Bathgate	D.S.C., R.D., R.N...
Surgeon......H. W. Case	*Purser*......J. W. Law...
Asst. Surgeon...M. Kirk Bryce	*2nd Purser*......H. H. Coop...
Chief Steward......	*Asst. Purser*....W. J. R. Jor...
	R. B. Powell

FROM
NEW YORK
TO
CHERBOURG AND SOUTHAMPTON
SATURDAY, MARCH 1, 1930

The Waites in Egypt 1930

While researching at the Berrien History Center in 2014 with my sister Lisa Marcato, I confirmed what I had believed: Dotte did not get on well with Lucretia Adams, her father's third wife. We discovered correspondence showing the Adams woman ensnarled in probate litigation with Dotte over the Barnes estate for twenty years. Lucretia Adams, in addition to receiving a stipend for life, took possession of the Territorial and Edwards homes, their contents and a nearby farm in Weesaw.

Dying in 1952, at age seventy-eight, Dotte witnessed the fencing in of America, the end of the traditional family farm, the last of the Potawatomi Indians and life-changing inventions. She enjoyed playing cards and the Gilded Age of sumptuous transatlantic travel. She looms large for me. A life well-lived. In our rapidly changing world today, I regularly return to that snow-white hair that seemed to hang suspended above Mimi's smiling, loving face.

CHAPTER 11

TENTH GENERATION
Michigan & California

Nurma Nadjy Ortland 1894-1972

Nurma Huesman, Waldorf Astoria Hotel, New York City, 1942

Child of Zella Dotte Barnes & Charles Ortland

Cracker

My grandmother, "Cracker" as we called her, was eighteen when she left her Benton Harbor home. It was 1912. She purchased a one-way ticket, boarded a train in Chicago, landing in Los Angeles, California, never to return to the cold Michigan winters. She would eventually convince her mother, Dotte, and Dotte's husband William Waite, to relocate to the sunshine state. My own California history starts with Cracker, three hundred years after my Ingersoll family history began in western Massachusetts in 1645.

My memoires of Cracker herself are vivid, but her stories about her life in Michigan, the Indians, and her Civil War grandparents remain elusive. Her Bel Air home, where I spent much of my childhood, was filled with breakfasts of buttermilk pancakes, afternoons pruning roses and gladiolas in her garden, and gin rummy and poker games before dinner. Sleeping in the room with the portrait of Maloan Barnes at the end of my bed, I think how different the lives of these two female ancestors were.

Cracker was always impeccably dressed in colorful silk dresses that "schussed." I remember that sound as she glided down the freshly waxed hallways in her matching high heel shoes. Her auburn hair coifed after her weekly hairdresser appointment, her lips covered in her favorite fuchsia lipstick, her matching fingernails. Her sapphire ring, the large jewel like a tiara on her finger. Maloan, on the other hand, wore cotton or ill-fitting linen dresses, mostly black, her hair flattened under her white-lace head cap. I imagine Maloan had callouses on her palms. Her portrait depicts a stern-looking, unadorned woman, with pursed lips and probably only a few teeth, indicative of a hard life.

Barnes Home, Territorial Road, Benton Harbor, Michigan

When Cracker arrived in southern California in 1912, Los Angeles was only a small town near the ocean. The surrounding hills were covered with citrus and olive fields. She would fall in love with Ralph Huesman and marry him in 1917, while the motion picture industry was still in its infancy. The silent movies of W.J. Griffith would soon be followed by the "talkies" with stars Charlie Chaplin, Douglas Fairbanks and William Powell. Many movie stars shopped at my grandfather's clothing store, Desmonds. I never tired of hearing Cracker's tales about glamorous Hollywood, sprinkled with subtle stories of her Michigan farm life.

How different her luxury Bel Air home was from her territorial home in Benton Harbor. Cracker and Ralph Huesman built a Spanish-style home designed by African-American architect, Paul

Rudolf. It had a panoramic view of downtown Los Angeles, before automobiles and smog. The house was located on the fifth fairway of the Los Angeles Golf and Country Club. In the backyard was a formal garden surrounded by an emerald green lawn. A bed of shockingly orange Birds of Paradise greeted you as you walked to the rear of her house. A grey stone pebble path directed you to the formal garden. Divided into twelve ilex box squares, each square was filled with one of my grandmother's favorite flowers: red California poppies, coral hollyhocks, purple irises and four varieties of roses. A long mixed row of avocado, lemon, orange and grapefruit trees bordered the southern end of the property with lance-shaped, silver-green leaves of a dozen giant eucalyptus trees bordering on the north.

Huesman Home, Bel Air, California

How fortunate I was to be born into this privileged family. Surrounded by the comforts of wealth, I never heard my grandmother say an unkind word about those of lesser means or of a different race. In fact, I never heard her discuss politics. She seemed to treat everyone with the same respect. I never heard a stereotypical slur come out of her mouth. Her black chauffeur, Henry Harris, drove my grandmother for twenty-eight years and was generously compensated when my grandmother died in 1972.

I'd like to believe the respect for others and moral values are in my Ingersoll genes. For nearly three centuries my ancestors were part of a time and history when European white settlers conquered and colonized America. They settled a nation whose founding was rooted in conquest, land expansion and profit. They and their peers displaced and relocated the indigenous people; found slavery acceptable or objectionable or tolerable, formulated in our ambiguous constitution, authored by our country's well-intentioned, brilliant, but bigoted founding fathers. Deaths caused from imported diseases and massacres are inexcusable. Land grabbing based on written agreements with a culture that did not read or write is unjust. Forced religious conversion is intolerable, and treating people of color as property to be bought and sold is unconscionable. Not treating women as equals is also unjust.

It's difficult to judge the past with standards of today. Each generation, each century, each decade is different. Intercultural relations, views and laws were constantly in flux, punctuated by wars and political and social setbacks as well as steps forward. Balancing the violent aspects of the country's origins against its triumphs is risky business. Taking the journey to discover my ancestral history was worth taking. I started in cemeteries, where the lives beneath the stones slowly revealed themselves, bringing to light the "story" that I belong in.

The End

CHRONOLOGICAL & GEOGRAPHICAL BIBLIOGRAPHY

MASSACHUSETTS: BOSTON, HARTFORD, NORTHAMPTON, & WESTFIELD

CHAPTER I - JOHN INGERSOLL

Anderson, Robert Charles. *The Great Migration: Immigrants to New England 1620-1640*. Boston: New England Genealogical and Historical Society, 2003.

Adams, James Russell, and Seth Pomeroy. *History of Northampton Massachusetts from its Settlement in 1654*. Northampton: Gazette Printing Company, 1898.

Adams, James Truslow. *The Founding of New England*. Boston: Atlantic Monthly Press Book, 1921.

Andrews, Charles. *Colonial Folkways*. New Haven: Yale University Press, 1920.

Andrews, Charles. *Our Earliest Colonial Settlements*. Princeton: Princeton University Press, 1933.

Avery, Lillian Drake. *The Ingersoll Family in America: 1629-1925*. New York: Frederick H. Hitchcock, 1926.

Banks, Charles Edward. *The Planters of the Commonwealth of Massachusetts- A Study of Immigration in Colonial Times: 1620-1640*. Boston: Houghton Mifflin Company, 1930.

Bridenbaugh, Carl. *Vexed and Troubled Englishmen, 1590-1642*. New York: Oxford University Press, 1968.

Coleman, R.V. *The First Frontier*. New York: Charles Scribner's Sons, 1948.

Colket, Meredith B. *Founders of Early American Families, Emigrating from Europe: 1607-1657*. Privately Published, 1975.

Copeland, Alfred M. *A History of Hampden County Massachusetts*. Boston: Century Memorial Publishing Co., 1902.

Cutter, William Richard. *Genealogical and Personal Memoirs Relating to the Families of Boston and Eastern Massachusetts*. New York: Lewis Historical Publishing Company, 1908.

Davis, Emerson. "A Historic Sketch of Westfield," *Westfield Athenaeum*, 1826.

Dewey, Louis, M. "Authentic History of Westfield," *Westfield Athenaeum*, 1865.

Drake, Samuel. "The Founders of New England, 1580-1643." *NEHGS Register Journal*, 1860.

Dunbar-Ortiz, Roxanne. *An Indigenous Peoples' History of the United States*. Boston: Beacon Press, 2014.

Dunn, Richard S. *Puritans & Yankees: The Winthrop Dynasty of New England 1630-1717*. Princeton: Princeton University Press, 1962.

Dwight, Timothy. *Travels in New-England and New-York*. London: William Baynes & Son Publishing, 1823.

Earle, Alice Morse. *Curious Punishments of Bygone Days*. New York: The Macmillan Company, 1897.

Earle, Alice Morse. *Home Life in Colonial Days*. New York: The Macmillan Company, 1917.

Earle, Alice Morse. *Stage Coach and Tavern Days*. New York: The Macmillan Company, 1900.

Ellis, George Edward. *The Red Man and the White Man in America, from its Discovery to the Present Time*. New York: Little, Brown & Co., 1882.

Everts, Louis. *History of the Connecticut Valley in Massachusetts*. Philadelphia: L.H. Everts & Co., 1879.

Farmer, John. *Genealogical Register of the First Settlers of New England*. Lancaster: Carter, Andrews & Co., 1829.

Flagg, Ernest: *Genealogical Notes on the Founding of New England, 1629-1640*. Hartford: Clearfield, 1926. Reprinted by Genealogical Publishing Co., 1970.

Goodwin, Nathaniel. *Genealogical Notes on the First Settlers of Connecticut and Massachusetts*. Hartford: F.A. Brown, 1856.

Greene, David. "The English Origin and Spiritual Turmoil of John Ingersoll of Westfield, Massachusetts." *NEHGS Register*, 1997.

Grenier, John. *The First Way of War, American War Making on the Frontier – 1607-1814*. New York: Cambridge University Press, 2005.

Harris, Edward D. *A Genealogical Record of Thomas Bascom and His Descendants*. Boston: W. P. Lunt, 1870.

Hawke, David Freeman. *Every Day Life in Early America*. New York: Harper & Row, 1988.

Holland, Josiah Gilbert. *History of Western Massachusetts - The Counties of Hampden, Hampshire, Franklin, and Berkshire*. Boston: Samuel Bowels & Co., 1855.

Hollister, G.H. *The History of Connecticut: From the First Settlers of the Colony to the Adaptation of the Present Constitution*. Hartford: L. Stebbins Publishing Company, 1855.

Hutchinson, Thomas. *The History of Massachusetts, from the first settlement thereof in 1628, until the Year 1750*. London: J. Murray, 1795.

Ingersoll, Thomas. *To Intermix with Our White Brothers: Indian Mixed Blood from Earliest Times to the Indian Removal*. Taos: University of New Mexico Press, 2005

Judd, Sylvester. The Judd Manuscript. Northampton: Forbes Library, 1789-1860.

Kneeland, F.N., and L.P. Bryant. *Northampton, the Meadow City*. Northampton: F.N Kneeland, 1894.

Leach, Douglas Edward. *Flintlock and Tomahawk: New England In King Philip's War*. New York: Macmillan, 1958.

Lockwood, Allison. "Finding Paradise: Northampton, Mass 1654-1861." *Daily Hampton Gazette*, 2004.

Lord, Kenneth. *Genealogy of the Descendants of Thomas Lord, an original proprietor and founder of Hartford*, Connecticut, in 1636. Privately Published, 1946.

Lockwood, John Hoyt. *Westfield & Its Historic Influences 1669-1919 - The Life of an Early Town*. Printed by the Author, 1922.

Love, William DeLoss. *The Colonial History of Hartford: gathered from the original records*. Published by the author, 1914.

Mathews, L.K. *The Expansion of New England: 1620-1865*. Boston: Houghton Mifflin Co., 1909.

McLean, Clara Chamberlain. *The Ingersoll Family*. Self-Published, 1903.

Ripley, Charles S. *The Ingersolls of Hampshire: a genealogical history of the family from their settlement in America, in the line of John Ingersoll of Westfield, Massachusetts*. Boston: Alfred Mudge, 1893.

Stiles, Chester D. *A History of the Town of Westfield*. Westfield: J.D. Cadle & Co., 1919.

Tepper, Michael. *Passengers to America*. Baltimore: Baltimore Genealogical Co., 1977.

Torrey, Clarence A. *New England Marriages Prior to 1700*. Baltimore: Genealogical Publishing Co., 1985.

Trowbridge, Francis Bacon. *The Ashley Genealogy. A History of the descendants of Robert Ashley of Springfield, Massachusetts*. Printed by the author, 1896.

Trumbull, James Hammond. *Memorial History of Hartford County, CT.* Boston: E.L. Osgood Publishing, 1886.

Trumbull, James Russell. *History of Northampton, Massachusetts, from its settlement in 1654.*

Northampton: Northampton (Press of Gazette Printing Company), 1898.

Truslow, James Adams. *A History of American Life & Provincial Society.* New York: The Macmillan Company, 1927.

Webster, William H. *History and Genealogy of the Governor John Webster Family of Connecticut.* Rochester: E.R. Andrews Printing Company, 1915.

Wolfe, Janet. "John Ingersoll's English Origins," *NEHGS Register*, 2012.

ONLINE & OTHER SOURCES

Connecticut State Library, Hartford
Dewey Research Center, Sheffield
Forbes Library, Northampton
Great Barrington Historical Society, Great Barrington
Great Barrington Public Library, Great Barrington
Hampton Gazette Newspaper: 1786-1843
Hartford Historical Society (HHS), Hartford
Massachusetts Historical Society (MHS), Boston
New England Historic Genealogical Society (NEHGS), Boston
The Mechanic Street Cemetery, Westfield
Westfield Athenaeum, Westfield

Westfield Historical Society, Westfield

Westfield Historic Commission, Westfield

AmericanAncestors.org

Ancestry.com

Archive.org

Bob Wolfe, University of Michigan

Florence Times

Hathi Trust Digital Library

Ingersoll.net

Janet Wolfe, University of Michigan

Massachusetts Gazette

NEHGS American Ancestors Journal

Northampton Gazette 1786-1890

WESTERN MASSACHUSETTS:

NORTHAMPTON, WESTFIELD, SHEFFIELD, & GREAT BARRINGTON, MA

CHAPTERS 2-5
THOMAS, MOSES, PETER & THOMAS 2ND INGERSOLL

Adams, James Truslow. *A History of American Life and Provincial Society - 1690-1763.* New York: Macmillan & Co., 1927.

Andrews, Charles M. *Colonial Folkways*. New Haven: Yale University Press, 1919.

Avery, Lillian Drake. *Genealogy of the Ingersoll Family in America*. New York: Grafton Press, 1926.

Axtell, James. *Beyond 1492: Encounters in Colonial North America*. New York: Oxford University Press, 1992.

Axtell, James. *The Invasion Within: The Contest of Cultures in Colonial America*. New York: Oxford University Press, 1985.

Carvalho III, Joseph. "Black Families in Hampden Co, 1650-1965." Hampden: NEHGS, 2011.

Cutter, William, R., *Genealogical & Personal Memoirs Relating to the Families of Massachusetts*. Chicago: Lewis Publishing Co., 1910.

Demos, John. *The Unredeemed Captive*, New York: Random House, 1995.

Drew, Bernard, A. *Henry Knox: The Revolutionary Trail in Western Massachusetts*. Jefferson: McFarland Publishing, 2012.

Dunn, Richard, S. *Puritans and Yankees: The Winthrop Dynasty of New England 1630-1717*. Princeton: Princeton University Press, 1962.

Ellis, Joseph J. *Revolutionary Summer*, New York: Random House, 2013.

Goodwin, Nathaniel. *First Settlers of Connecticut & Massachusetts*. Hartford: F.A Brown, 1856.

Ferguson, John. *Memoir of the Life and Character of Rev. Samuel Hopkins*. Cornhill: Leonard, W. Kimball, 1830.

Kelly, Jack. *Band of Giants*. New York: St. Martin's Press, 2014.

King, David C. *The Indians of the Berkshires*. Troy: Troy Book Makers, 2014.

Leach, Douglas Edward. *Flintlock and Tomahawk: New England In King Philip's War*. New York: Macmillan, 1958.

Lockwood, Rev. John. *Westfield and Its Historic Influences – 1669-1919*. Published by the author, Westfield, 1922.

Mathews, Lois, K. *The Expansion of New England: 1620-1865*. Boston: Houghton Mifflin Co., 1909.

Miles, Lyon G. *A life of John Konkapot : the Mohican chief who sold his Berkshire hunting grounds to Puritan settlers...* New Marlborough: Historical Society of New Marlborough, 2009.

Morgan, Edmund S. *American Heroes*. New York: W.W. Norton & Co., 2009.

Puls, Mark. *Henry Knox, Visionary General of the American Revolution*. New York: Macmillan Co., 2008.

Richter, Daniel, K. *The Ordeal of the Longhouse: The People of the Iroquois League in the Era of European Expansion*. Chapel Hill: University of North Carolina Press, 1992.

Ripley, Charles, Stedman, *The Ingersolls of Hampshire*. Boston: Alfred Mudge & Son, 1893.

Stelzer, Alice Plouchard. *Female Adventurers: The Women Who Helped Colonize Mass & Conn*. Cambridge: Merrimack Media, 2013.

Stuart, Nancy Rubin. *The Muse of the Revolution: The Secret Pen of Mercy Otis Warren*. Boston: Beacons Press, 2009.

Taylor, Alan. *American Colonies: The Settling of North America*. New York: Penguin Books, 2001.

Taylor, Alan. *American Revolutions, A Continental History, 1750-1804*. New York: W.W. Norton, 2016.

Taylor, Charles, J. *History of Great Barrington, Berkshire County, MA*. Barrington: Clark W. Bryan & Co., 1882.

Trowbridge, Francis, B. *The Ashley Genealogy: History of the Descendants of Robert Ashley of Springfield, Mass*. New Haven: For the Author, 1896.

Truslow, James, Adams. *A History of American Life & Provincial Society -1690-1763*. New York: Macmillan Co., 1927.

Ullmann, Helen, S. *Western Massachusetts Families in 1790*. Boston: NEHGS.

Stuart, Nancy, R. *The Muse of the Revolution - The Secret Pen of Mercy Otis Warren and The Founding of a Nation*. Boston: Beacon Press, 2008.

Puls, Mark. *Henry Knox: Visionary General of the American Revolution*. New York: Macmillan, 2008.

Webster, William Holland. *The History and the Genealogy of the Governor John Webster Family of CT*. Rochester: E.R. Andrew Printing Co., 1915.

ONLINE & OTHER SOURCES

AmericanAncestors.org

Archive.org

Ashley House, Ashley Falls

Bridge Street Cemetery, Northampton

Dewey Research Center, Sheffield

Forbes Library, Northampton

Great Barrington Historical Society

Great Barrington Office of Registry & Deeds

Great Barrington Public Library

Hadley Burial Ground, Hadley, MA

Hampshire County Probate Files, Sheffield, 1751, Box 77, p77-8:1)

Hampshire Registry

Hathi Trust Digital Library

Ingersoll.net

Massachusetteshistoricalsociety.com

Mechanic Street Cemetery, Westfield

Mission House, Stockbridge

NEHGS: American Ancestors Journal

NSDAR.org

NSDAR: American Spirit Magazine

NYGBS: New York Genealogical & Biographical Society

Stockbridge Library & Museum, Stockbridge

Wainwright Inn, Great Barrington

SOUTHWESTERN MICHIGAN:

BUCHANAN, BENTON HARBOR & NILES

CHAPTERS 6-9
CALEB & MALOAN INGERSOLL, JOHN ELI & JOHN EATON BARNES,
MALOAN INGERSOLL BARNES & ZELLA DOTTE BARNES

Alger, M.W. *Benton Harbor: The Metropolis of the Michigan Fruit Belt.* Benton Harbor, 1915.

Barnes, Trescott, C. *The Barnes Family Year Book.* New York: The Grafton Press, 1907.

Bellesiles, Michael A. *1877 - America's Year of Living Violently.* New York: The New Press, 2010.

Canton, Bruce. *The Civil War.* New York: Houghton Mifflin Co., 1960.

Chapman Brothers. *Portrait & Biographical Album of St. Joseph County.* Chicago: Charles C. Chapman & Company, 1889.

Chapman, Charles. *History of St. Joseph County.* Chicago: Charles C. Chapman & Company, 1880.

Cleland, Charles. *Rules of Conquest: The History and Culture of Michigan Native Americans.* Detroit: University of Michigan Press, 1992.

Coolidge, Judge Orvillle. *20th Century History of Berrien County.* Lewis Publishing Co., 1906.

Johnson, Robert Underwood. *Battles and Leaders of the Civil War.* New York: The Century Company, 1887.

Daniel, Larry, Shiloh-The Battle that Changed the War. New York: Simon & Schuster, 1997.

DeHart, Richard P. *Past and Present of Tippecanoe* County. Indianapolis: B.F. Bowen & Co., 1909.

Dempsey, Jack. *Michigan and the Civil War: A Great and Bloody Sacrifice.* Charleston: History Press, 2011.

Goodspeed Brothers. *Pictorial and biographical memoirs of Indianapolis and Marion County, Indiana, together with biographies of many prominent men of other portions of the state, both living and dead.* Chicago: Goodspeed Brothers, 1893.

Howard, Timothy, Edward, *History of St. Joseph County.* Chicago: The Lewis Publishing Co., 1907.

Johnson, Crisfield. *History of Berrien Co & Van Buren Co.* Philadelphia: Ensign D.W. & Co., 1880.

MacPherson, Myra. *The Scarlet Sisters: Sex, Suffrage & Scandal in the Gilded Age.* New York: Barnes & Noble, 2014.

Meyers, Robert, C. *Greetings from Benton Harbor.* Berrien: Berrien County Historical Association, 2005.

Meyers, Robert, C. *Greetings from Buchanan.* Berrien: Berrien County Historical Association, 2011.

Morton, J.S. *Reminiscences of the Lower St. Joseph River Valley.* Benton Harbor: Federation of Women's Clubs.

Robertson, John. *Michigan in the War.* Lansing: W.S. George & Co., 1882.

Shaara, Jeff. *A Blaze of Glory*. New York: Ballantine Books, 2012.

Shea, William, L., and Terrence J. Winschel. *Vicksburg is the Key*. Lincoln: Univ. of Nebraska Press, 2003.

Winchester, Simon. *The Men Who United the States*. New York: Harper Collins, 2014.

Woffen, William. *Biographical & Historical Sketches of Early Indian*. Indianapolis: Hammond & Co., 1883.

ONLINE & OTHER SOURCES

1883 Atlas of Berrien County, Michigan

Benton Harbor Public Library, Benton Harbor

Berrien County Journal (1878)

Berrien County Record (1869)

Berrien Springs History Center, Berrien Springs

Buchanan Masonic Lodge, Buchanan

Buchanan Public Library, Buchanan

Centerforhistory.org

CountyHistoryPreservationSociety.com

Friends of Oak Ridge Newspaper, Oak Ridge

Harpers Ferry Armory & Museum

IndianaHistoricalSociety.org

Michigan History Magazine

Niles Public Library, Niles

NSDAR Algonquin Chapter- Benton Harbor

Oak Ridge Cemetery, Buchanan

SeekingMichigan.org

Shepherdstown, West Virginia Historical Museum

The Docket, Newsletter, The History Center, Berrien Springs The News Palladium

CHAPTER 8: JOHN ELI BARNES & ANNA ROSS (WEST) BARNES

Aler, F. Vernon. *Aler's History of Martinsburg & Berkeley Company.* Self-Published, 1888.

Barnes, George Newton. *Barnes Genealogy and Family Records.* Self-Published, The Rieg & Smith Printing Co., 1903.

Barnes, Trescott, *The Barnes Family Yearbook.* New York: Grafton Press, 2007.

Bushong, Millard Kessler. *A History of Jefferson Co. 1719-1940.* Baltimore: Heritage Books, 2009.

Cartwell, Thomas K. *Shenandoah Valley Pioneers and Their Descendants: History of Frederick Co. from its Formation 1738-1908.* Westminster: Heritage Books Inc., 2007.

Evans, Willis. *History of Berkeley Co., West Virginia.* Baltimore: Heritage Books, 2001.

McSherry, James. *The History of Maryland from Its 1st Settlement 1634-1848.* Baltimore: J. Lucas & E.K Deaver, 1837.

ONLINE & OTHER SOURCES

Berkeley Co. Historical Society, Martinsburg

Berrien Co. History Center, Berrien Springs (Probate File)

Jefferson Co. Historical Society, Charlestown

Jefferson Co., Historical Society Magazine, Charleston

Historical Society of Frederick Co. Frederick

Potowac Guardian

Martinsburg Gazette

Rumsceian Society, Shepherdstown

ACKNOWLEDGEMENTS

I have met so many wonderful people while researching and writing this book, it's hard for me to single out just a few. I am especially grateful for the assistance of Taos poet, writer and teacher Veronica Golos; staff at the New England Genealogy and Historical Society in Boston, who patiently answered all my questions; staff at the Westfield Athenaeum Library; the Dewey Research Center in Sheffield at the Great Barrington Historical Society; The Great Barrington Office of Registry; the Stockbridge Historical Museum and Mission House and the Forbes Library in Northampton.

Gravestone preservation workshops led by Southampton Historian Zachary Studenroth and conservators Joel Snodgrass and Jonathan Appell convinced me to track down the stories beneath the stones. Special thanks to Westfield, Massachusetts cemetery historian Robert Dewey, Westfield Historic Commission Cindy Gaylord, and Northampton DAR Karen Trato and her husband Larry who drove me up to the Hadley Historic Cemetery where Larry found the gravestone for my thirteenth-generation great-grandfather, Governor John Webster.

I received equally warm welcomes in southern Michigan. Robert D. Brown took me right to the Barnes family plot at Three Oaks Cemetery in Buchanan and then helped my sister Lisa and I navigate the microfiche at the Buchanan District Library. Robert Myers pulled out dust-covered century-old cardboard boxes at the Berrien Springs Historical Center. At the Benton Harbor Public Library, DAR Regent Faye Chamberlain of the Algonquin DAR Chapter, (which my great grandmother Zella Dotte Barnes belonged to), helped locate Barnes newspaper clippings. Heartfelt thanks go to my deceased Michigan family friend Mary Jane Dillon and her daughter Johanna, who shared endless Barnes and Ingersoll family stories over casseroles and wine.

My visit to Shepherdstown, West Virginia did not reveal any new information about the senior John Barnes' unknown parents, but I did get a flavor of the beautiful Harpers Ferry river town and surrounding rolling countryside. The curator of the Shepherdstown Historical Museum showed me the Barnes boat that showcased the first steam engine for George Washington and General Lafayette.

My visit to West Cornell, Connecticut this past October was a final treat as I drew near completion of my book. I met with two Ingersoll descendants, Thomas Ingersoll of Sheffield and Ian (John Ingersoll the 10th) of West Cornwall. Ian carries on the tradition of fine furniture and cabinetry making. Tom, a professional landscaper and musician, surprised us with the original Ingersoll hand-inked genealogy chart.

Although I never met Janet Wolf, another Ingersoll descendant and genealogy expert from the University of Michigan, we spoke on the phone and emailed. Finally, I want to thank Laurna Toti who provided me with research on the Eaton and Banes families; Gerry Hausman, children's history writer, editor, and publisher; and *Shelter Island Reporter* staff member Archer Brown, who diligently proof read my manuscript.

To all the above and those I have not mentioned, who preserve our written history in our historical societies, museums, and libraries, and preserve the stone records in our burial grounds. Thank you.

Made in the USA
Coppell, TX
20 January 2021

48516321R00083